Join with LaRouche

Fire the Whole Top Stratum of the FBI!

Feb. 18—In a discussion today, Lyndon LaRouche highlighted the significance of the call being widely raised to dump the entire (mis-) leadership of the FBI after the latest in its series of bloody fiascos.

It wouldn't have taken much of an "investigation." Alarmed citizens had given the FBI not one, but two completely specific, credible tips that Nikolas Cruz would massacre high school students exactly as he did on Feb. 14. And if the FBI had bothered to mount any investigation at all in response, it would also have found, long before the killings, a third, additional warning that some journalists found within two days afterwards: that Cruz belonged to an "Instagram" chat group where he made similar threats. He showed off his "arsenal" of seven guns, and wrote, "I think I am going to kill people."

President Trump tweeted yesterday, "Very sad that the FBI missed all of the many signals sent out by the Florida school shooter. This is not acceptable. They are spending too much time trying to prove Russia collusion with the Trump campaign. There is no collusion. Get back to basics and make us all proud."

Florida GOP Gov. Rick Scott also called the FBI's response to the second tip "unacceptable," and called for Director Wray's resignation. "We constantly promote 'see something, say something,' and a courageous person did just that to the FBI. And the FBI failed to act. 'See something, say something' is an incredibly impor-tant tool, and people must have confidence in the follow-through from law enforcement. The FBI Director needs to resign."

Not just the Director. Judge Jeanine Pirro, the Fox News commentator who is a former prosecutor and judge, argues rightly and with passion that the entire top echelon of the FBI must be removed. Any fiasco of this magnitude in any corporation would force the resignation or removal of all the top officers and the board of directors. The utter failure shown here by the FBI is so monumental that this rule must apply here.

The FBI could not be bothered to investigate before the massacre, but afterwards, it had the *chutzpah* to go before television cameras to lie that the Facebook post reported in September, which had Nikolas Cruz' name on it, was insufficient to establish a "positive identification." Not only did they have the name, but in fact, Facebook collects additional data to facilitate such identification.

But is this the first such total failure? What about 9/11? And then, we know that Russia had given the FBI warnings about the Boston bombers. Judge Pirro says she knows that serial abuser Larry Nassar had been on the FBI's radar screen for years. Fiasco after fiasco. She says that there are honest men and women in the FBI, but they are sidelined and denied promotion by top management. The entire top echelon must go. Her ten-minute statement yesterday is worth watching.

EIR Contents

www.larouchepub.com Volume 45, Number 8, February 23, 2018

EIRNS/Stuart Lewis

Cover This Week

Lyndon LaRouche, addressing a LaRouche Youth Movement educational in 2005.

JOIN WITH LAROUCHE

In our previous, Feb. 16 issue, we reprinted Lyndon LaRouche's "ON THE NOETIC PRINCIPLE: Vernadsky and Dirichlet's Principle," of May 18, 2005. The sequel to that paper was "THE SUBJECT OF PRINCIPLE: Project 'Genesis,'" of March 14, 2008, which we had intended to reprint in this issue. Instead, we printed the article above for the occasion of the 200th anniversary of the birth of Frederick Douglass. "Project 'Genesis'" will follow in our next issue.

Memo to the U.S.A. on Japan's Infrastructure Success

by Daisuke Kotegawa

Mr. Kotegawa had a 32-year career in Japan's Ministry of Finance. He was IMF Executive Director 2007-2010.

Feb. 10—In the United States, there is currently an intense debate underway on the issue of infrastructure. Having learned about the Hamiltonian approach to national banking from the American Occupation Army after the Second World War, Japan established the Fiscal Investment and Loan Program, which played a major role in the rebuilding of the war-ravaged Japanese economy.

Since Japan did not benefit from a Marshall Plan, we mobilized Post Bank savings and government pension funds as a major source of financing. While the ministries in charge of these funds preferred independent management, the Ministry of Finance, with the support of the powerful General Headquarters (GHQ) of the American Occupation Force under General Douglas MacArthur, established the "integrated management" of the Fiscal Investment and Loan Program by the Ministry of Finance. In addition, the Ministry of Finance oversaw the national budget, and established tax policies. This system of comprehensive management of the three major sources of credit for economic recovery was critical. It enabled a maximum utilization of the limited credit sources towards the objective of restoring the national economy.

Over the period of 50 years, from 1951 to 2001, the Fiscal Investment and Loan Program accumulated extensive experience and understanding of the most effective use of funds for the reconstruction and mainte-

nance of different elements of the national infrastructure grid. This included a differentiated understanding of how to recover costs of construction, based on user charges and other revenue sources.

I was in charge of the program at its peak in the late 1980s and early 1990s, and learned a great deal from that experience. I offer the following observations and recommendations for my American friends, as they proceed to design and implement an urgently needed infrastructure program.

Economic vs. Financial Returns

The first critical point in designing an efficient program for government-assisted infrastructure investment is the need to differentiate between *financial returns* and *economic returns.*

A commercially viable project has sufficient positive financial returns to warrant private investment and

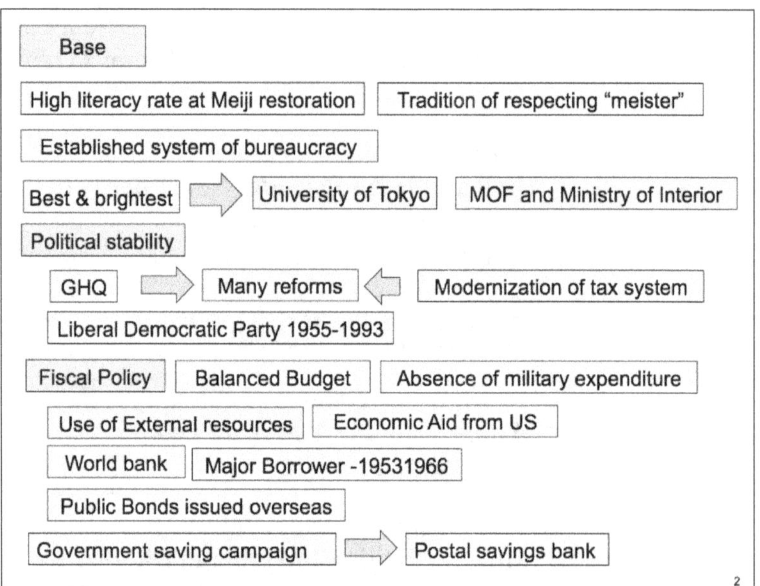

commercial loans as a means of financing. A good example is an airline business, which provides a vital transportation infrastructure service, on a busy route.

There are projects which are not commercially viable but which deliver positive economic returns for the general public and can contribute to an overall increase in economic efficiency and real growth over time. A good example is a ring road around an urban area. Such a modern highway is of great economic benefit, but the fees do not provide a sufficient financial return, therefore making the project not commercially viable. But such projects are economically viable and are appropriate for public financing.

Market fundamentalists argue that only financially viable projects are legitimate, and therefore "soft loan" programs involving government funding and loan guarantees are never justified. This is false. Take the example of an urban subway system. While investments to increase capacity, through the development of double-tracking or the construction of new lines may be commercially viable if increased ridership fees are large enough to justify commercial investments, on the other hand, the additional costs of investment in new subway cars, improved air conditioning, etc., although clearly beneficial to the general public, and are a source of increased productivity, do not represent commercially profitable investments at all. These are good examples of infrastructure needs that are best served by soft-loan programs based on government assistance.

Public-private partnerships (PPPs) can work for commercially viable projects but they are not appropriate for projects that are only economically viable. The frequently cited case of the New Jersey Turnpike as an example of a successful PPP is relevant. The New Jersey Turnpike is heavily used by commuters, long-haul trucks, and passenger cars, which pay sufficient tolls to cover depreciation costs on the initial investment, as well as operating costs. Other instances of PPPs being used to pay for highway projects, such as the Indiana toll road, failed be-

---

FILP's Role in the Growth

Early years of post-war recovery (until mid-1950s)

➢ Focused on fund provision to industrial plant and equipment investment
  • Helped reconstruct four prioritized industries
    • Shipbuilding
    • Coal
    • Steel
    • Maritime
  • Utilized post-war financial aid from the United States
➢ Established FILP agencies amid the recovery (next slide)
➢ With World Bank loans, 31 projects of infrastructure development were implemented (1953 – 1966).
  - Bullet Train ("Shinkansen")   - Steel works
  - Highways ("Tomei" and "Meishin") - Hydroelectric dam ("Kurobe" dam)

What is FILP?

"Fiscal Loan and Investment Program"

• FILP utilizes financial techniques to bring together interest-bearing funds and the FILP agencies in the most effective and efficient way.

FILP

Fiscal Loan Fund
Source for fiscal loans. The purpose is to integrate and manage funds raised based on the sovereign credit.

FILP Plan
List of reserved amounts for each FILP agency with respect to each fiscal year's FILP.

FILP Agencies
Government-affiliate institutions which are consist of those execute projects and those make loans.

Grant Funds (Tax) and Loan Funds (FILP)

[Scheme of Flow of Funds in General Account Subsidies] (Grant funds) (i.e. Toll-free roads)

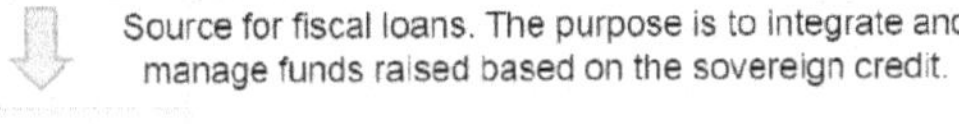

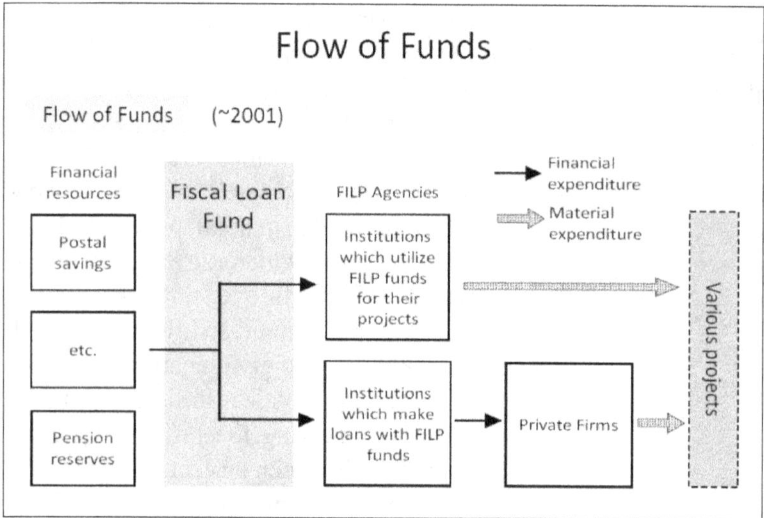

cause they are not able to generate sufficient toll revenues to cover the costs of commercially financed improvements.

During a period when privatization was gaining great popularity, Argentina won praise from the International Monetary Fund for President Carlos Menem's privatization of much of the state sector economy. Those privatization measures ultimately failed, and led to foreign takeovers and other consequences that damaged the interests of the Argentine people. The general welfare was damaged by the over-zealous privatization program. The Menem government failed to see that privatization was only one of a number of options for financing infrastructure, and it led to failure.

Failure to properly understand which projects are commercially viable and which are economically viable has led, in recent instances, to the intervention of vulture funds and the further decline in the welfare of the nation.

Effective political leadership must be based on a commitment to the general welfare. Such politicians can successfully argue for taxpayers' investment in infrastructure on the grounds that the economic benefits of such investments are worthwhile and will improve the conditions of life.

PPPs, in general, can be successful in areas of dense population where there are large numbers of users who are prepared to pay for services. In contrast, it is extraordinarily difficult to identify PPP projects that can work in rural areas. Unless government-assisted investments are made in those areas that are not viable for PPPs, the gap in levels of needed infrastructure between urban and rural areas will grow.

Special Measures for Infrastructure Investment

The expected service-life of infrastructure projects like roads, bridges, and tunnels is 50-60 years. Borrowing money now, whether through commercial or government-assisted loan programs, is justified because the benefits to current and future generations from the improved infrastructure are greater than the costs of construction and maintenance in real economic terms.

Bonds for infrastructure projects can be issued at low interest rates when they are guaranteed by the government. These bonds can be equal to the yields on Treasury Bonds. The current low interest rates offer an excellent opportunity for large-scale infrastructure investment, as borrowing costs are at an historic low. In addition, the excessive liquidity in the market, created by the post-2008 quantitative easing programs of the

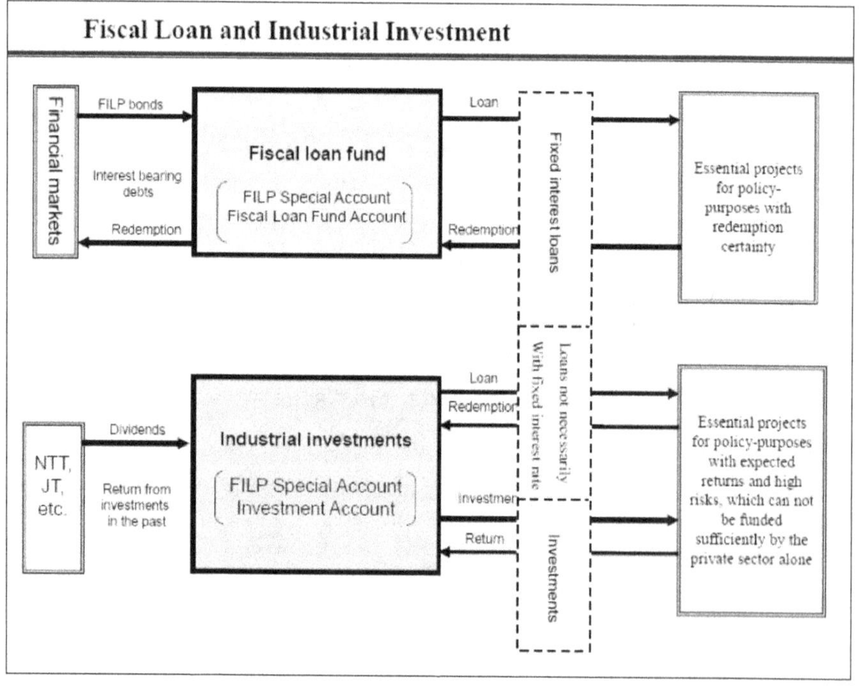

Background

1. History of FILP before WWII (-1945)
   - Concept of Fiscal Loan Fund was created in 1870's, since private financial institutions were not developed.
   - The investments resulted in a huge loss when the war was over.
2. The Fiscal Loan Fund Act (1951)
   - Respond to demands for long-term funds for post-war reconstruction
   - Three objectives are specified:
     - United Management of state funds
       - Postal savings, Pension reserves and etc. were required to deposit the Fiscal Loan Fund
     - Investment of funds in secure and efficient ways
       - The recipients of loans are limited to the government, local governments and government related institutions that are fully owned by the government.
     - Contribution to the promotion of public interest

Federal Reserve and Treasury, can be channeled into infrastructure investments, rather than being used for bailouts, stock buy-backs, derivatives and other speculative activity.

Infrastructure expansion and improvements create large numbers of productive jobs, and will boost household wealth and overall GDP growth. This is an instance where Keynesian stimulus can be effective, by reducing the unemployment rate, increasing disposable income and stimulating national economic growth. The risks to governments providing the new sources of investment are minimal compared to the benefits, if the infrastructure programs are properly conceived and managed.

In those instances where infrastructure investments cannot be paid for out of projected user fees, tax revenues can justifiably be used for financing. The use of such tax revenue sources was successful in Japan, when rural railroad lines were improved through double-tracking and expansion. This approach is also effective during periods of economic downturn, in which government-assisted loans can be secured by the future tax revenues that will come after the economy recovers.

Arguments Against Government Funding

Instead of increasing general tax rates, infrastructure construction in the United States can be financed by special-entity bonds, earmarked for infrastructure projects. With government guarantees, the bonds will be low yield. Such "infrastructure bonds" would be attractive to financial institutions, both domestic and foreign. They have the added advantage that they are investments in future economic growth, while regular Treasury bonds finance current operations. Increases in government debt associated with infrastructure bonds are not a burden, because they will grow the economy, and generate increased wealth and tax revenue. This is not the case with other government bonds, which cover operating costs and do not contribute to future economic growth.

While the United States does not have the equivalent of Post Bank savings and large public sector pension funds, this does not preclude efforts on the model of Japan's successful Fiscal Investment and Loan Program. A national infrastructure bank, authorized to issue infrastructure bonds secured by Federal govern-

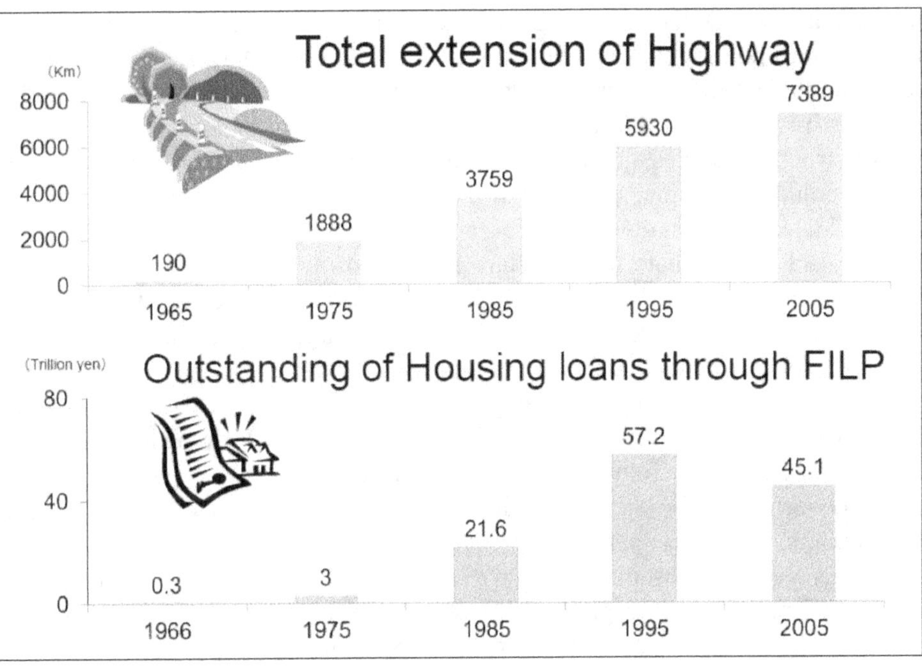

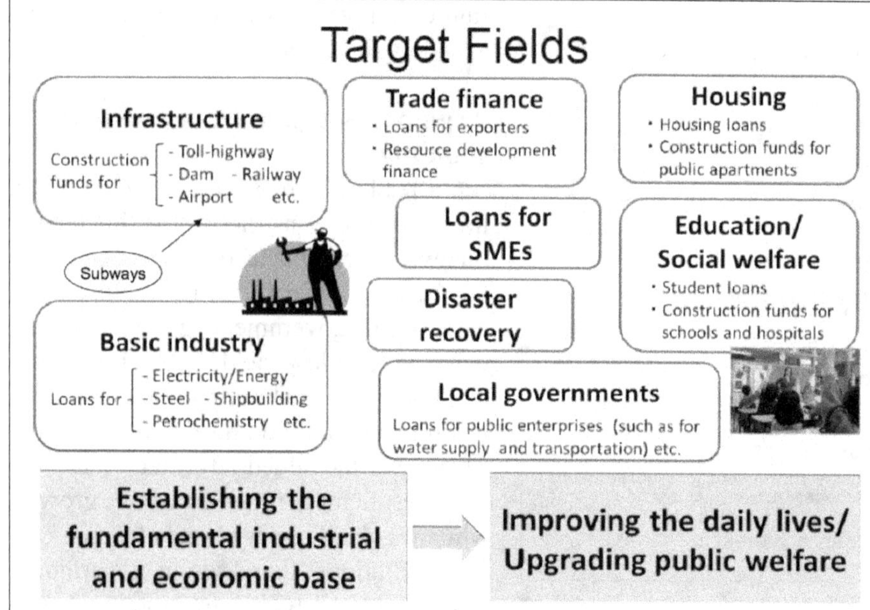

ment guarantees, would be attractive investments for individual retirement accounts, mutual funds, and private-sector pension programs. They would be as attractive for foreign investors as U.S. Treasury Bonds.

The continuing position of the U.S. Dollar as the world's leading currency is a further reason that the United States can launch a large-scale infrastructure investment program without fear of speculative attack. At the same time, however, the Obama Administration's sanctions against Russia have somewhat eroded the status of the U.S. Dollar, as nations wishing to maintain trade with Russia are seeking alternatives to U.S. Dollar-denominated transactions, to avoid possible asset seizures. If the United States continues to adopt such self-destructive policies, the strong position of the U.S. Dollar could, over time, erode. That could open the United States to speculative attack.

The lack of adequate infrastructure investment in the United States over recent decades has led to a reduction in potential GDP growth. Consider the following example: Amtrak trains take three hours between Washington and New York City, with frequent delays. The distance between Washington and New York is equal to the distance between Tokyo and Nagoya. The bullet train between those two Japanese cities takes one-and-a-half hours, and trains operate every seven to ten minutes. This creates a substantial amount of economic activity, spurring economic growth. Improved Amtrak service between Washington and New York would in-

crease the GDP of the United States. Such investments in other parts of the United States would produce the same increases in GDP.

Infrastructure investment in underdeveloped areas of the country spurs economic growth and new enterprises. Investment in infrastructure in these "new frontier" areas reduces costs of business expansion. Even a once-deserted area can be revitalized with new infrastructure, which would provide a better business environment at a lower cost. This would further close the gap between rich and poor.

Flood control and sewage management were important elements of Japan's Fiscal Investment and Loan Program. Power companies can make use of beneficial low-interest loans with long maturity to build dams and other vital water projects at lower costs. Protection of vital assets from natural disasters is a national priority, and timely investment in infrastructure reduces costs from natural disasters.

Flood control programs benefit agriculture, which suffers in the western United States from obsolete systems of irrigation. Demand for agricultural products is expected to increase rapidly, with the rise of Asian and African states as modern economies. The United States must be prepared to boost agricultural production with the assistance of improved infrastructure.

Concerns that Chinese investments in U.S. infrastructure bonds would give China increased political leverage over the United States are largely unfounded. Investments in infrastructure bonds allow for Chinese investment with less leverage than ownership of critical infrastructure.

Japan's experience of half-a-century of postwar investment in infrastructure offers important lessons for those planning out the new U.S. infrastructure investments and methods of implementation. Given that the United States played such an important role in the immediate postwar recovery of Japan, which employed methods first developed during the formative years of the United States, these lessons should be readily adopted in the present U.S. efforts.

China's New Silk Road and Europe

GBTIMES is a multimedia news site based in Finland, where it was founded by Chinese entrepreneur Zhao Yinong, which refers to itself as a "bridge between China and the rest of the world." It published the introduction below and the following interview with Helga Zepp-LaRouche on Feb. 16.

screenshot from GBTimes

Chinese high-speed rail is a central part of the the New Silk Road project.

China's ambitious plan to link itself with Europe and Africa through new Silk Road trade routes has so far received a mixed welcome in Europe.

The Belt and Road iInitiative (BRI), the brainchild of Chinese President Xi Jinping, proposes to boost trade and economic integration across Eurasia through over $1 trillion worth of investments in railways, ports, power plants and other infrastructure links. The BRI has been officially endorsed by Central and Eastern European countries, many of which are hoping that Chinese investment could create jobs and improve infrastructure.

But Western European countries have been more cautious, with British Prime Minister Theresa May declining to sign up to the BRI during her recent trip to Beijing and French President Emmanuel Macron warning during his trip to China that the New Silk Road cannot be "one-way." There are also concerns in Brussels about a lack of reciprocity in trade with China and increasing Chinese investment in critical infrastructure in Europe.

The German-based Schiller Institute, however, has for the past several years been campaigning for the Belt and Road Initiative in Europe by organizing hundreds of conferences on the topic. Helga Zepp-LaRouche, the institute's founder and president, talked to gbtimes.com about the initiative and why she believes Europe should embrace it.

Q: What is the Schiller Institute?

Helga Zepp-LaRouche: The Schiller Institute was founded in 1984 as a think tank, with the main idea behind it being that peace and order in the world would only function if each nation would relate to the best cultural tradition of the others and vice versa.

One of its focuses was to fight for a just new world economic order, something like in the tradition of the Nonaligned Movement, especially inspired by the ideas of my husband, Mr. Lyndon LaRouche, and secondly to fight for a renaissance of classical culture. I gave it the name of [German philosopher] Friedrich Schiller because his image of man was the most noble and beautiful one and I thought such a conception was urgently needed in the political realm.

Q: How did you first get to know China?

Zepp-LaRouche: I went to China for the first time in 1971 on a cargo ship, which was repaired in Shanghai. So, I had plenty of occasions to visit many factories, children's palaces, and the countryside. I also went to Shenzhen, Qingdao and Beijing, and that left a very lasting impression on me because this was in the middle of the Cultural Revolution (1966-1976) and China was very much different then. But it started a deep interest on my side in Chinese philosophy and culture.

EIRNS

The opening of the Beijing International Symposium on Economic Development of the Regions Along the New Euro-Asia Continental Bridge, 1996.

I was also inspired by the changes which took place in China after the reforms of Deng Xiaoping. I visited China many times in the 1990s and the 2000s, and especially after Xi Jinping announced the New Silk Road. And I could see the dramatic changes and the economic miracle which China has undergone. I feel very privileged that I have sort of personally witnessed the unbelievable transformation of China over almost 50 years.

Q: You mentioned President Xi Jinping who proposed the Belt and Road initiative in 2013. The Schiller Institute has been very supportive of the BRI. Why is this?

Zepp-LaRouche: First, the Belt and Road Initiative is presently the most important strategic initiative on the planet because it proposes what Xi Jinping calls a community for shared future of humanity. The idea of one humanity is a perfect conception for overcoming geopolitics, which was the reason for two world wars and which, in the age of nuclear weapons, can lead to a terrible catastrophe just as big. If you look at the incredible progress this initiative has made in the five years since it was announced, you already see a tremendous transfor-

mation where the developing countries in Africa, Latin America and Asia, for the first time, have legitimate hope to overcome poverty and under-development.

It just so happens that the Belt and Road initiative is very much in accordance with proposals my husband and myself have made during the last decades. After the Soviet Union disintegrated in 1991 we proposed something that we called the Eurasian Land-Bridge, which was the idea to connect the Eurasian peoples and industries through development corridors. The Chinese government picked up on the proposal to organize an international conference in Beijing in 1996, in which I participated as speaker. Already at that point China considered the development of the Eurasian Land-Bridge a strategic initiative, but this was put on hold due to the Asian financial crisis of 1997. We were then extremely happy when Xi Jinping announced this policy in 2013. With China's economic power all these plans can now be realized.

Q: Why do you think the Chinese are interested in this idea of bridging the Eurasian continent?

Zepp-LaRouche: China has developed its own economic model of lifting its population out of poverty and it also wants to contribute to eliminating poverty on the world scale. I think that is a very different approach to many other countries. There are now only 30 million poor people left in China. In comparison, there are 90 million poor people in the European Union and more than 50 million people who are officially poor in the United States, but no clear plans to eliminate poverty in totality.

Q: So, you are saying China is currently the only major country that has a global vision?

Zepp-LaRouche: Yes. I participated in the Belt and Road forum in Beijing last year and everyone who participated in this conference had a distinct impression that we were witnessing the beginning of a new era of mankind.

At the Oct. 18-24, 2017 19th National Congress of the Chinese Communist Party, Xi promoted the goal of having a fully developed, modern, culturally advanced, happy country by 2050—not only happiness for the Chinese people, but for all the people in the world. Normally, politicians in the West think at best until the next election, and I have not heard from any Western leader a plan on how to uplift the entire human species in the next 30, 40, 50 years.

The idea to create happiness for the people as a policy goal was last heard during the American Revolution when it was established in the American Declaration of Independence that it is a fundamental right to have life, liberty, and the pursuit of happiness. This is a notion coming from Leibniz, which means the ability of people to develop their full potential. I have seen in China on many occasions that people there really think that way. They have the idea that there is no limit to their ability to self-perfect to improve society and relations between nations. It's a completely different spirit to what you find anywhere in the West.

Q: All Central and Eastern European countries have officially joined the Belt and Road Initiative, but many Western countries including the UK, France and Germany have been more cautious about it. Why do you think this is the case?

Zepp-LaRouche: When certain politicians in these

Xinhua/Li Tao

China President Xi Jinping visiting Yangling Village on July 18, 2016.

countries say they want to insist on standards and rules, and that they don't want the spreading of Chinese investment in Europe, I think it's a question of geopolitical control. The EU for example could have developed Central and Eastern Europe, the Balkans, but they didn't. When China then comes and starts to build the kind of infrastructure that the EU did not build, these countries are happy and want to go with the New Silk Road. And that causes some people who believe in geopolitics to see it as a threat.

The present Western system is based not on the common good as a primary orientation, but on monetarist profit-making. This system benefits those who speculate and those who run the banking system. But it leads to such things like the 2008 financial crisis, which was a systemic crisis, and nothing has been done since other than quantitative easing and pumping money.

Q: But do you think China itself has overcome geopolitics?

Zepp-LaRouche: I know that that is not the view of many politicians in the West, but I think assumptions about China are just people's projections of what they themselves think. I am not a naive person—I have studied this in depth and looked at it closely—and I do think that China does not plan to dominate the world with its system. The Chinese model is more attractive, and many countries want to repeat what it has been doing, but I don't think China wants to impose its values.

My explanation for this is China's Confucian tradition. For example, Christians are supposed to win other people over to Christianity, but Confucianism does not do that. Confucianism is perfectly happy to live in co-existence. And if you look at the entire history of China, you never had religious war. You had Buddhism, Confucianism, Taoism and Christianity all living in a perfect ecumenical harmony. So, I think in Chinese history, you don't find anything which would give credibility to the claim that China is not doing what they say. I think they are doing exactly what they say they are doing and they mean it.

Q: What would it mean for Western European countries to join the Belt and Road Initiative?

Zepp-LaRouche: It would mean that there would be a shift towards the real economy. Right now, you have this money-makes-money philosophy, but if you look at even an advanced country like Germany, there's a tremendous backlog in infrastructure. There are warnings by some of the logistic organizations that Germany is about to lose its standard as a location for industrial development because of the collapse of the infrastructure. So, if European countries would join the New Silk Road it would mean that they could basically renew their infrastructure like China has done, and build high-speed trains connecting all major cities.

With the policy of the Troika (the European Commission, the European Central Bank, and International Monetary Fund), the industries and the economies of the Southern European countries were destroyed. Now you see that with the advantages that come from Chinese investment in the Piraeus port and other projects in Greece, it's going upwards. And with the EU, it went downwards. The same is true for Italy, Spain and Portugal.

Europe could also participate with China in the reconstruction of Southwest Asia, of Syria, of Iraq, because you must bring economic development to these countries if terrorism is supposed to be eliminated. You have to give young people a future which they don't have right now. It would mean you could solve the refugee problem in a human way.

Q: But do you think that some Europeans might be cautious about the growing Chinese influence because they think they might have to someday accept the same kind of restrictions on freedoms that China has at home?

Zepp-LaRouche: Yes, but if people are worried that they may lose some of their hedonistic impulses—

well, that might not be altogether such a bad thing. Because what we are seeing right now is a decadent society with all the violence, pornography and drug addiction. You have an opium epidemic in the United States, which is contributing to the fact that life expectancy is going down for the first time. If there is any parameter for the functioning of an economy, it is the life expectancy. If an economy is doing well, it's increasing and obviously it's an indicator that there is something fundamentally wrong if it's going down because of suicide, alcoholism and drug addiction.

On the other hand, there was just a poll made in Germany among 42 firms which were taken over by Chinese investors. In all cases, the management and the employees said that it was a positive thing that the Chinese took over, instead of speculators or hedge funds. I think some of these changes that come with more Chinese investment and influence would be beneficial. I would even go so far to agree with Leibniz, who said already in the 17th Century that because of the superior morality of the Chinese, one should import Chinese missionaries to teach morality to the Europeans.

Q: So, you are optimistic that the acceptance of the Belt and Road Initiative is growing in Europe eventually?

Zepp-LaRouche: We have found that all people who do business in China or who have travelled to China or who are married with a Chinese person, are all positive, and they know that what China is doing is a historic transformation of humanity.

The Belt and Road Initiative is not just about economics; it's not just about infrastructure from A to B, but it is really a new paradigm. And what I mean by new paradigm is a new way of understanding the role of humanity. We are the only creative species who can invent new technologies and sciences and change the mode of our existence. It's not the nature of man to be greedy, to chase for stock market gains and try to exploit and dominate others. It's the nature of man to develop our own potential to the fullest so that we can contribute to the development of the human species. And the new paradigm will be that more and more people, as time goes by, will be able to realize their true potential as human beings.

https://gbtimes.com/interview-with-helga-zepp-la-rouche-on-chinas-new-silk-road-and-europe

On the Anniversary of John Glenn's Orbit

by Kesha Rogers

Feb. 20—This week we celebrate America's first orbital flight, the orbit of the Earth by American astronaut John Glenn, 56 years ago on Feb. 20, 1962. Glenn's flight was not merely an isolated event in the history of space exploration; it propelled America's space program to the forefront of science, to the Moon and beyond. John Glenn was a member of the first class of American astronauts, the Mercury 7, who were presented to the American people and the world on April 9, 1959 only one year after the founding of the National Aeronautics and Space Administration (NASA) in July of 1958. This year we happily celebrate the 60th Anniversary of NASA!

Astronaut John Glenn, using a photometer to view the Sun during sunset from from the Friendship 7 Mercury spacecraft on Feb. 26, 1962.

America's Foothold in Space

By the time NASA had announced its first class of astronauts, the Soviets had already taken a lead in space. America faced a great challenge with the successful launch of the first Sputnik satellite into orbit on October 4, 1957. America's first successful satellite, the Explorer 1, was launched on January 31, 1958, under the leadership of the great space pioneer and rocket scientist, Wernher von Braun, after a series of failed attempts dubbed "flopniks." With the successful launch of America's first satellite, we had, in the words of von Braun, "firmly established our foothold in space." Within four years of that first satellite launch, we succeeded in our first manned orbit.

The United States took up the space race with a national commitment, visionary leadership, and determination to unleash a new era in space exploration, dedicated to the advancement of human progress under the direction of President Kennedy. His vision for propelling America's space program forward could not have been done with cheap, profit-making private schemes and commercialization of space, but rigorous research and development, and robust federal funding. That is

how we overcame the Soviet lead in space; they had already launched two satellites, a dog, and the first human being, Yuri Gagarin, who orbited the Earth on April 12, 1961.

The American space program had to take a new leap forward, and it did. After a great wave of optimism swept the nation with the launching of the first suborbital mission by Mercury astronaut Alan Shepard on May 5, 1961, President Kennedy set forth a new vision that would change the course of history for the United States and the world in the direction of space exploration. On May 25, 1961, President John F. Kennedy delivered an historic speech before a joint session of Congress which would set us on course to the Moon with American astronauts by the end of the decade. Kennedy's ambitious program would not be accomplished cheaply, nor was it to be a fly-by-night cheap race to some distant finish line just to plant a flag. He unleashed a national mission that mobilized the best and greatest of our nation's talents, and offered a col-

President John F. Kennedy puts forward the goal of sending an American safely to the Moon before the end of the decade, before a joint session of Congress, May 25, 1961.

such work increased the productive standards of living of the American people. Those who want to subject society to the idea of limits to growth, limited resources, anti-growth and impeding the creative progress of all human minds certainly despised the vision laid out by President Kennedy and carried out by many great pioneers in the exploration of space.

The forty- year-old Mercury astronaut John Glenn, on Feb. 20, 1962, became the first American to orbit the Earth in his Friendship 7 spacecraft. His flight, as were the flights of others who flew before, and after him, was not part of a publicity stunt to get us to the Moon and back. Those space missions were the leading edge of a long-term vision for the future of mankind. President Kennedy's 1961 vision to "land a man on the Moon and return him safely to Earth," by the end of the decade, was the major first step in advancing what space pioneer Krafft Ehricke described as mankind's "extra-terrestrial imperative," to become a galactic species. Ehricke rejected the ideas of limits to growth.

laborative "win-win" ending to the Cold War. In that 1961 message, he called for an extended set of goals including the launching of a Rover Nuclear Rocket and advanced weather satellites. Meeting Kennedy's challenge and that vision for the American space program created great leaps in economic and scientific progress, propelling not only our nation forward, but advancing the whole of mankind. That was the real intention of the space program and why so many would dedicate their lives to such a mission, even at the risk of losing their own lives.

Those who paved the way did not do it to enhance the profits of a small group of greedy fat cats; they put their talents to work to address the problems confronting our nation and the whole of mankind. This passion for scientific discovery and its application in outer space is precisely what those who so vehemently oppose the progress of the space program feared then, and still fear today—the fear of the optimism and joy it carries with it, and the unimpeachable fact that

Becoming a Galactic Species

President Kennedy outlined a broad plan for human space exploration, to the Moon and beyond. He recognized the importance of weather monitoring and fore-

John Glenn entering the Friendship 7 Mercury capsule on Feb. 20, 1962.

Krafft Ehricke with his space station model.

casting, with an array of satellite systems, and moving to atomic rockets for more advanced propulsion, including missions to Mars. Kennedy increasingly saw the necessity to end the Cold War threat of mutually assured destruction, and in 1963 put forward a plan for a joint landing on the Moon with the Russians. Soviet Premier Nikita Khrushchov reversed his initial rejection of this proposal, according to reports from his son, Sergei Khrushchov. To the great misfortune of mankind, Kennedy was killed and the USA stepped into the quagmire of Vietnam.

Krafft Ehricke had an even more thoroughly developed blueprint for how mankind as a species would transition away from the "winner take all" geopolitics of the Cold War, to mutually beneficial "win-win" collaboration among nations. He developed this concept in what he called an Open World paradigm. By adopting the cultural optimism of his Three Laws of Astronautics, nations of the world could start on a path to growth, with many beneficial results:

• An increase in new technologies, which would result from an increase in our scientific understanding of the physical laws governing the universe;

• A decrease in the entropy of our economic systems, by utilizing the new technologies developed, which allow the use of new and better resources, as would fusion energy;

• The improvement of international relations among nations, lessening the causes of war;

• The improvement of internal relations within nations, lessening the causes of civil strife;

• The stabilization of population growth in a life-oriented direction;

• The preservation of the biosphere, and a fuller understanding of its interaction with the solar and galactic environment;

• The expansion of the human species to bring cis-lunar space into our economic grasp;

• The exploration of deep space from permanent science labs on the Moon;

• The protection of life from extreme space weather, and potentially hazardous asteroids and comets;

• A deeper understanding of the origins of our Galaxy, Solar system, and life itself;

• The ability to protect humanity, and all species, from extinction.

The continued expansion of human civilization beyond Earth is imperative for pulling people out of poverty on Earth. When we choose to explore the stars, planets, moons, comets, asteroids, and electromagnetic environment, we force ourselves to develop new technologies, materials, scientific breakthroughs, and cultural pride. These improvements allow us to better feed, educate, employ, and keep healthy the entire world. In a message to a Memorial Conference in honor of Krafft Ehricke titled, "Colonize Space! Open the Age of Reason," American statesman Lyndon LaRouche paid tribute Ehricke, stating "Our dear Krafft

The Three Laws of Astronautics

From Krafft Ehricke's 1957 "Three Fundamental Laws of Astronautics":

First Law: Nobody and nothing under the natural laws of this universe impose any limitations on man except man himself.

Second Law: Not only the Earth, but the entire Solar system, and as much of the Universe as he can reach under the laws of nature, are man's rightful field of activity.

Third Law: By expanding through the Universe, man fulfills his destiny as an element of life, endowed with the power of reason and the wisdom of the moral law within himself.

Ehricke served with notable distinction, to the degree that his name must be remembered most prominently by those who construct the first colonies on the Moon and Mars. He has helped in an important and practical degree, to make clear to humanity, that it has been the intent of the Creator that mankind's destiny is to become mankind in the Universe." Our deep exploration of the planetary, solar, and galactic space in which we live, is the basis for how we come to better understand and care for ourselves and each other, and improve the overall quality of human life and our biosphere.

NASA is not merely a line item in a budget; it is the most advanced driver of human progress currently in existence. The full funding of NASA and with it the revitalization of the idea of mission, as presented and implanted under President Kennedy, is no mere relic, but it is the basis for human survival in the Solar system we inhabit.

This fundamental resource, the human space program, which is critical for progress, cannot rely on funding from unreliable sources, such as short-term fiscal budgets, Wall Street markets, or public-private partnerships. It needs a funding source which will remain undeterred by the shifting sands of popular opinion, a source based on understanding long-term goals and designed to fulfill those goals. Full funding of NASA's mission for human progress requires a National Bank with a capital budget.

A national bank, as conceived originally by our first Treasury Secretary Alexander Hamilton, can issue credit on a long-term basis (5- to 50-year terms) at low, fixed interest rates (1-2% APY) for the purpose of funding research and development of entirely new technologies and scientific principles, which will rapidly increase the productive viability of humanity. The purpose is not to generate profits from the credit issuance itself, but for the credit to fund the breakthroughs that improve society through the dissemination of new discoveries and inventions in every sector including, but not limited to, medicine, agriculture,

EIRNS/Marsha Bowen

Kesha Rogers, Houston, Texas, Feb. 10, 2018.

materials, communication, transportation, machine tool design, and education. That type of approach generated a 10:1 real profit from the Apollo Program alone, and also permanently increased the standard of living in thousands of ways, everything from velcro to incredible advances in nuclear medicine.

Unlike the Federal Reserve, which issues currency only to maintain the reserves of the largest "too big to fail/jail" banks (and issues quantitative easing when their speculative bubbles pop), a Hamiltonian National Bank's purpose is to involve the general population, as well as local, state, and federal banks, in funding the creation of our long-term future. The bank would be capitalized by receiving federal tax revenue, long-term Treasury bonds, municipal and state bonds, and commercial deposits, and would issue credit specifically for large-scale projects of a national and international scope.

By issuing currency backed by Treasury securities for specific projects designed to upgrade economic efficiency and physical productive output, the bank effectively creates technologies and infrastructure. Those projects "pay for themselves" in the long term, but may take several years to mature.

Eliminating the uncertainty of funding for flagship missions in space exploration and energy development—missions to include bringing the Moon into the economic grasp of mankind and developing fusion energy from the extensive Helium-3 in the lunar soil—will dramatically accelerate the goal of eliminating poverty, both domestically and worldwide. Let us advance the true cause of exploration and the development of mankind in the Universe as Krafft Ehricke understood so well, and as Lyndon LaRouche has continued to put at the forefront of the fight for human progress in the development of space, saying "There in the stars, lies mankind's entry into the long awaited Age of Reason, when our species sheds at last the cultural residue of the beast."

Kesha Rogers is an independent candidate for Congress in the 9th Congressional District in Texas.

Belt and Road Provides New Energy to Pakistan Development

by William Jones, *EIR* Washington Bureau Chief

Feb. 17—The China-Pakistan Economic Corridor is one of the most ambitious elements of the Belt and Road Initiative. In addition to the major transportation corridor— stretching from Kashgar in the most westerly part of China's Xinjiang region through the mountains of northeast Pakistan, all the way south to the Indian Ocean port at Gwadar— China is also providing new sources of energy to the Pakistan economy. One of these is a major hydropower project near the capital of Islamabad, the Karot Hydropower Station.

The project is presently employing 18,000 Pakistani workers in the construction this massive plant with the help of the masters in the field, the China Three Gorges Corporation, or rather its subsidiary, the China Three Gorges South Asia Investment. It cut its teeth on the massive Three Gorges Dam in China in the 1990s. The project also employs 460 Chinese workers, whose primary task has been to train the Pakistani workers. Before the construction is finished, it will probably have as many as 3,500 workers employed, of which 85% will be from Pakistan. The first power unit will be connected to the grid in 2021.

When it is completed, the 720-megawatt power plant is projected to produce 3.2 billion kilowatts of electricity per hour. This is the energy equivalent of burning 1.5 million tons of coal in one year. Pakistan has long suffered from power outages. Even in Islamabad, the capital, power outages are quite common. During the Summer, the duration of blackouts can last up to 12 hours a day. The Karot plant is the first such plant to be financed by the Silk Road Fund, which was announced by President Xi in December 2014, to help finance projects along the Belt and Road.

The dam will be located near the villages of Karot in

Suki Kanari hydropower station under construction, another project of the China-Pakistan Economic Corridor in Pakistan.

Punjab and Hollar in Azad Jammu and Kashmir, which is roughly 55 km south-east of Islamabad. The dam is expected to be 95.5 meters high and 460 meters wide, across the Jhelum River. The hydropower project will have a reservoir storage capacity of 164.5 million cubic meters at full supply level, and is expected to cost approximately $2 billion. The reservoir is expected to stretch approximately 27 km upstream of the dam at 461 meters above sea level. The surface powerhouse, consisting of four turbines, will be situated approximately 650 meters downstream of the dam crest, and 300 meters upstream of the Karot Bridge.

The project will also include four 316-meter headrace tunnels, a spillway, three 447-meter diversion tunnels, and coffer dams upstream and downstream of the main dam. The plant will be interconnected to the national grid by means of a 5 km, 500 kV transmission line. Power generation will operate for six months a year.

The Karot Power Company, of which Three Gorges is the majority shareholder, will operate the dam for 30 years, after which it will be turned over to the Pakistan government.

Mueller Indictments of Russian Social Media Trolls Scam the American People

by Barbara Boyd

Feb. 18—In the first two weeks of February, things looked really bad for the coup being run against the President of the United States. Congress, in the form of the House Intelligence Committee, announced that it would be publishing a series of three memos exposing how the coup was fomented. If the first memo—which was published on Feb. 2, concerning a deliberate fraud on the Foreign Intelligence Surveillance Court by former FBI Director James Comey, former Deputy Attorney General Sally Yates, and others—is any guide, criminal investigation of the Obama White House is on the agenda.

The House Intelligence Committee, backed by members of the Senate Judiciary Committee, has announced that two upcoming memos will expose the role of key State Department personnel and Obama's intelligence chiefs, respectively, in the coup. The track being followed by Congressional investigators is centered on the use of a very dirty dossier about Donald Trump produced by British intelligence agent Christopher Steele, as part of a full-spectrum British/Obama information warfare operation designed to defeat Donald Trump in the 2016 election. Failing that, the British and Obama set out to poison Trump's presidency and impeach him.

Senators Chuck Grassley and Lindsey Graham had already referred Steele to the U.S. Department of Justice for criminal prosecution. Therefore, something, obviously had to be done to turn the tables or, at least, slow the charge against the coup plotters. Something had to be done to take the focus away from the actual British criminals and their U.S. co-conspirators, and re-furbish the increasingly discredited "Russiagate" myth. Enter the ever-dutiful Robert Mueller III and his flimsy Feb. 16 indictment of 13 Russians and 3 Russian companies which allegedly conspired to interfere in the 2016 U.S. election.

A few things of note are already visible right on the surface of this case. The indictment, written and formulated like a press release rather than a legal document, will never have its factual basis challenged in court. Mueller knows this. The U.S.A. has no extradition treaty with Russia, and the Russian constitution bars extradition of Russian citizens. According to Deputy Attorney General Rod Rosenstein, the Russians fooled the Trump campaign by pretending to be Americans, by using stolen identities. There is no allegation of "collusion" with the Trump campaign. There is no claim that this operation affected the vote in the Presidential election, nor could there be, as the expenditures alleged for this amateurish hit-or-miss social media operation were completely dwarfed—by huge orders of magnitude—by the expenditures made by Hillary Clinton, Donald Trump, and Bernie Sanders, and associated PACs and organizations.

But, oh those evil Russian "bad actors" who "meddled" in an American election, as even the President initially tweeted. As we have repeatedly demonstrated, the strategic context of the coup against Trump is an all-out effort to preserve the Anglo-American order against what is perceived to be the rising power of China, now allied with Russia. China has constantly and persistently invited the United States to join its Belt and Road Initiative, the largest infrastructure development project ever undertaken in world history. President Trump's reasoned approach to both Russia and China is seen as an existential threat to the continued Anglo-American partnership, which has dominated the world since Franklin Roosevelt's death.

Russiagate's initial narrative, that Russians hacked the DNC and John Podesta's email accounts to damage the Clinton campaign and elect Donald Trump, has been discredited by the work of the Veteran Intelligence Professionals for Sanity (VIPS). William Binney of the VIPS, who is a former technical director of the NSA, states that if such Russian hacking occurred, the NSA would have the evidence, and would have found a way to produce it. The VIPS also conducted a scientific experiment demonstrating that the source of the Wikileaks DNC emails was a leak, not a hack. Now, the emphasis has shifted to another claim in the January 2017, evidence-free "assessment," of supposed Russian interference by three of Obama's intelligence chiefs—this assessment claims that the Russians ran a social media campaign designed to support Bernie Sanders and Donald Trump, and later to roil the existing divisions in American society. This social media campaign was allegedly run from an entity called the Internet Research Agency (IRA) in St. Petersburg, Russia, according to the 2017 Obama intelligence assessment and Mueller's indictment.

Mueller claims that from 2014 forward, the IRA, financed by two companies owned by Russian oligarch Yevgeniy Prigozhin, planned and implemented a campaign to interfere with the 2016 U.S. Presidential elections as part of a project named "translator." According to Mueller, the campaign involved phony Facebook groups, and phony Twitter, Instagram, and email accounts, all run by Russians from the IRA who had stolen

EUROPE

Yevgeny Prigozhin, Russian Oligarch Indicted by U.S., Is Known as 'Putin's Cook'

By NEIL MacFARQUHAR   FEB. 16, 2018

screenshot from New York Times

Yevgeny Prigozhin (left) and Russia President Vladimir Putin (center).

six U.S. identities to facilitate the operation. They used Facebook's paid advertising feature, according to Mueller, to boost their posts; two IRA employees visited the U.S. under false pretenses to gather intelligence; contacts were made with the Trump campaign's state offices and field organizations to coordinate social media, and set up rallies in Washington D.C., New York, Florida, and Pennsylvania. Allegedly, the IRA sought to suppress the black vote by bogus social media posts, and also claimed that the election was "rigged" on Clinton's behalf. After the election, the IRA engaged in the same social media and rally activities to both support Trump and to support the "Resist" movement seeking Trump's impeachment.

I will leave it to others to document the obvious U.S. hypocrisy concerning the premise of Russiagate. The United States has intervened in elections all over the world, repeatedly, and, as former CIA Director James Woolsey recently said on Fox News, for the "good of those nations." When someone is elected whom we don't like, like Victor Yanukovych in Ukraine, we simply launch a coup using such native assets as neo-Nazi shock troops (Ukraine) or Al-Qaeda and other Islamic terrorists (Syria). Obama's White House, in the form of the National Security Council's Ben Rhodes, claimed that it conducted information warfare operations with finesse, setting up, for example, a media echo-chamber to sell the Iran nuclear deal based on the fact that most reporters were "27-year-old kids who knew nothing."

The indictment's own overblown allegations should subject it to ridicule. How do we know that Yevgeniy Prigozhin is the boss of this operation? According to Mueller, an IRA employee took a picture of himself in front of the White House on Prigozhin's birthday with the sign, "Happy Birthday, Boss." The amazing Russian sleuths found out the startling fact—from one their American social media contacts—that they should concentrate on "purple states." And the indictment contains an email from one of the allegedly savvy conspirators stating, "We had a slight crisis here at work: the FBI busted our activity (not a joke). So, I got preoccupied with covering tracks together with colleagues . . . I created all these pictures and posts, and the Americans believed that it was written by their people." Despite the IRA's allegedly broad mandate to disrupt American politics, the only U.S. political campaign they attempted to directly contact and compromise appears to be the campaign of Donald Trump.

Rewarmed British Gruel Behind the Indictment

The story of how the IRA came to be an infamous "Putin-controlled troll farm" in the narratives of Western intelligence is an old and long one. We can say, definitively, that it is rewarmed British gruel, a British lie as poisonous as Christopher Steele's dirty dossier.

At the beginning of 2014, an anti-Russian group of hackers, initially called "The Anonymous International," and later, "Shaltay-Boltay," claimed that the building at Saint Petersburg, Savushkina 55, housed a troll farm run by the Kremlin.[1] Since then, this building has been photographed and highlighted endlessly by MI6, all of the British press and tabloids, the CIA, the FBI, NATO, the BBC, the State Department's propa-

screenshot from the Guardian

cc/Mitya Alesh Kovskiy

Mikhail Khodorkovsky at first press conference after being released from jail, Dec. 22, 2013.

ganda departments and NGOs, CNN, and most of the rest of the mainstream American media. Infiltration operations have been run and publicized by the same people. Actions against the alleged IRA have been filed by infiltrators in the Russian courts. Any intelligent observer would ask the first obvious question: Why, if this building and the alleged company occupying it has been so repeatedly targeted by Western intelligence, would Putin be stupid enough to run an influence operation from that location targeting the 2016 elections? The answer should be obvious—he did not.

The allegation made by "Anonymous International" was immediately picked up by Mikhail Khodorkovsky, an anti-Putin oligarch who collaborates in multiple ways with both British and U.S. intelligence. His Institute for Modern Russia is a major conduit of U.S. information warfare operations into Russia. The "Anonymous International" allegations were also immediately leaked to *BuzzFeed*, the same publication used thereafter to make the dirty British Steele dossier against Donald Trump a very public document.

---

1. A very intriguing and detailed account, from a Russian perspective, of the Western intelligence links to the Russian troll farm in Mueller's indictment is provided by "Scott Humor" at the Saker blog.

A major escalation of British and U.S. information warfare operations against Russia occurred in 2014. According to *Politico* magazine, Hillary Clinton threw a fit at that time about the inadequacy of Anglo-American information-war operations selling the Ukraine coup. The British, Obama and his CIA and State Department, and their Kiev regime allies, were equally adamant about the necessity for heightened operations on this front. The joint British-Obama Administration-NATO initiative known as the Strategic Communications Service, based in Latvia, was activated to counter *any* Russian version of events. The St. Petersburg social media troll farm at the center of Mueller's indictment has been a staple of this campaign, endlessly photographed, infiltrated, and written about by Western information warriors from 2014 onward.

A huge and well-funded anti-Putin "information warfare" industry now operates in Washington, D.C., featuring the Atlantic Council's Digital Forensic Research Lab, where none other than Dmitri Alperovich (author of the "Russia hacked the DNC" hoax) is a fellow; the Alliance for the Defense of Democracy; the German Marshall Fund; the Information Warfare Initiative of the Washington Center for Policy Analysis; the National Endowment for Democracy; and the State Department's propaganda arms, Radio Free Liberty and Radio Free Europe. Generous funding has been provided by the likes of Khodorkovsky and George Soros. As the result of the National Defense Authorization Act signed by Obama in 2016, millions of dollars are now flowing into this U.S. information warfare initiative.[2] All of these entities have been integral to the coup against President Trump.

According to "The Saker" blog's Russian account of the IRA,[3] the company itself does not exist. It is a fiction created by Shaltay-Boltay, the successor to "Anonymous International" in conjunction with western intelligence agencies. Shaltay-Boltay, Russian for "Humpty-Dumpty," conducted a systematic campaign of hacking, leaking, and extortion against Russian officials, according to accounts of its own activities published in the *Guardian*. Members of Shaltay-Boltay were arrested in November 2016 together with rogue Russian FSB officers said to control their activities. All were charged with treason by the Russian government, specifically some form of collaboration with the U.S.A. The British account of this affair, produced in the Feb. 9, 2017 *Guardian*, claims that the treason charges were based on the hackers and rogue FSB officials having confessed their trolling crimes to the CIA. According to a November 2017, Radio Free Europe/Radio Liberty article, the FSB "cyber" division where the arrested officers worked, had been in collaboration with U.S. law enforcement agencies for years.

While So-Called Democrats Impose Censorship in the U.S.A.

The final ironic twist I will cite concerning Mueller's indictment, is the fact that the pre-packaged information it has imported from British intelligence has been and is being used to support wholesale censorship in the United States. On Nov. 30, 2016, an anonymous group called "Prop or Not," in conjunction with the *Washington Post*, published a list of U.S. publications it accused of being Russian propaganda fronts. The list included practically any publication which had doubted the "official" version of events concerning September 11, 2001, the ensuing Iraq war, or the Russiagate myth created by the Clinton Campaign and the Obama Administration. "Prop or Not" is traceable to the same information war specialists behind the Russian Troll Farm story at the center of Mueller's indictment.[4] Facebook, Twitter, and all the social media platforms, are now on the lookout to censor dissenting views right out of their platforms, the First Amendment to the Constitution of the United States be damned.

This is a product of the McCarthyite hysteria infecting our Congress and literally destroying the mental capacities of many. It is endlessly stoked by the national news media—a phenomenon far more dangerous to the national security of the United States than any ham-handed Russian operation to "meddle" in our elections. It is that hysteria and madness which now mistakes Russian puppy postings on Facebook for an attempt to steal the American mind. The late Robert Parry wrote passionately about this in his last days and warned us. It would be a fitting tribute both to him and ourselves if we moved now to finally end this insane British coup.[5]

2. See https://consortiumnews.com/2018/01/28/unpacking-the-shadowy-outfit-behind-2017s-biggest-fake-news-story/ and the three-part series by George Eliason in *Consortium News*: Part 1, Part 2, Part3
3. http://thesaker.is/a-brief-history-of-the-kremlin-trolls/

4. https://consortiumnews.com/2018/01/28/unpacking-the-shadowy-outfit-behind-2017s-biggest-fake-news-story/
5. https://consortiumnews.com/2017/09/28/the-slimy-business-of-russia-gate/ and https://consortiumnews.com/2017/11/06/learning-to-love-mccarthyism/

How the British and Obama Diddled the United States

by Barbara Boyd

Feb. 18—On Sept. 29, 2017, *Executive Intelligence Review* published the original version of the dossier "Robert Mueller is An Amoral Legal Assassin: He Will Do His Job If You Let Him." To date, that dossier, now being circulated nationwide by LaRouche PAC, represents the most thorough and the most accurate assessment as to the character of Robert Mueller, as well as the utterly fraudulent nature of the ongoing treasonous effort to bring down the Trump Presidency.

This present report is an update to that dossier, with the emphasis on the dramatic significance of two documents which were released in the first days of February. The first is the House Intelligence document known as the "Nunes Memo," and the second is the—by far more substantive—un-redacted document authored by Senators Grassley and Graham.

We shall examine the importance of these two documents in depth, as well as significant other developments which flow from the impact of their release. Before doing so, however, it is of critical importance that a matter of primary overriding concern be re-stated here, at the beginning of this update.

cc/Sarah Burris

President Barack Obama and Hillary Clinton at the Democratic National Convention, July 27, 2016.

The British Origin of the Coup

Nothing of any truth about the current assault on President Trump can be understood, unless one addresses the question of *why* all of this is occurring, along with the subsumed question of *"cui bono?"* This requires transcending the world of partisan politics and inside-the-beltway gossip, and the necessity for examining the *strategic* setting and implications surrounding the coup plot.

Everything that is now transpiring must be viewed within that truthful strategic context. During the eight years of the Obama presidency, and the prior Administration of George W. Bush, a profound shift in U.S. strategic policy took place. Obama, working closely with—and often under the direction of—the British, committed the United States to enforcing a global policy of Anglo-American hegemonism, what is sometimes referred to as a "uni-polar world." This took the form of escalating provocations against Russia, and more recently the targeting of China. Currently, this imperial Anglo-American faction is determined to thwart China's gigantic Belt and Road Initiative infrastructure development of

Eurasia, Africa, Southwest Asia (the Middle East), and nations in Central and South America. This largest infrastructure development project in human history now involves more than 68 countries.

For the British, such geo-political designs are nothing new. British strategic policy since before World War I has been based on geopolitics. Under the theories of Lord Halford Mackinder, completely embraced by today's Anglo-American foreign policy establishment, control of Eurasia dictates strategic mastery of the world. China is now establishing vast transportation and other infrastructure throughout Eurasia, a region which Anglo-American policy up until now had reserved as a primitive looting ground.

Unable to break from imperial axioms and join China's offer of win-win cooperation, let alone offer a viable alternative model which promotes the general welfare, Barack Obama and the British adopted a strategy of geopolitical containment and provocation, a New Cold War policy. It began with the Anglo-American coup in Ukraine in 2014, pushing NATO right up to Russia's borders, and involves hostile encirclement strategies against both Russia and China, employing color revolutions, economic sanctions, overt economic, cyber, and information warfare, provocative military maneuvers, development of new nuclear and other warfare capacities, and military support of insurgents and terrorists in states friendly and/ or trading with Russia or China, such as Iran and Syria. All of this, of course, threatens the extinction of the human race.

In November 2016, it was the intention of Obama and the British that Hillary Clinton would continue this dangerous geo-political gambit. Donald Trump's victory in that election stopped this mad drive to war just as it was turning very hot.

As we detailed in our original Mueller dossier, "Russiagate,"—which has roiled our nation since Summer 2016, has driven most members of Congress into a McCarthyite insanity so severe that you can literally picture them braying at the Moon at night, and has critically undermined Donald Trump's presidency—has absolutely nothing to do with any hostile action by Russia against the United States. Its origins are to be

found in the desperation of the British and American establishments, among individuals and interests who are frantic to re-impose the strategic outlook of the Obama Administration.

The Nunes Memo: Unraveling a British Fraud

Let us begin by examining the so-called Nunes Memo, a four page document by U.S. Representative Devin Nunes (R-Calif.), which was released to the public Feb. 2, 2018. That Memo concerns the documented fraud on the FISA Court by the DOJ and FBI in obtaining surveillance of Trump foreign policy volunteer Carter Page. That fraud involved the DOJ/FBI use of a dirty dossier claiming ties between Trump and Russia, a dossier which was authored by British intelligence agent Christopher Steele. Steele, we now know, was working simultaneously for the FBI, MI6, and Hillary Clinton's campaign, while providing salacious and bogus copy about Russia and Trump to numerous U.S. journalists. Steele told the journalists he was working with the FBI and other intelligence agencies to wrap his fake cash-for-trash allegations in an aura of legitimacy. He told the FBI he was not speaking to journalists and was reporting to the FBI out of a sense of duty and patriotism.

According to the Nunes Memo, the Obama Justice Department and James Comey's FBI affirmatively misrepresented what they knew about Christopher Steele's operation to the FISA Court and, instead, touted his credibility in order to obtain surveillance of a U.S. citizen, Carter Page, and the Trump campaign. The Page FBI surveillance was then used to feed a media frenzy based on a magical mystery tour of mainstream media by British Intelligence Agent Steele. The big lie generated, that Trump was a compromised agent of Vladimir Putin, became the theme of the last months of Hillary Clinton's presidential campaign, Clinton having paid for the bogus claim lock, stock, and barrel, with Obama's CIA Director John Brennan fanning the British lie.

Steele's dirty dossier was not only used to abuse the FISA law and attempt to swing an American election. It was and is the centerpiece of the entire FBI counterintelligence investigation of Trump and Russia—the subject that Robert Mueller is supposedly diligently investigating.

Far from being a competent intelligence product, Steele's composite of 17 memos written from June through December 2016, is a British fraud, a hoax, an amateurish hodgepodge created and deployed for British strategic purposes. After more than 20 months of intense investigation, few, if any of its claims have panned out. Even former FBI Director James Comey admits that its claims are "salacious and unverified." To take but one example, the claim that Donald Trump romped with Russian prostitutes in Moscow on a bed used once by the Obamas (Steele's most depraved and salacious offering), appears to be the product of a drunken bar conversation between two wannabe hustlers, Sergei Millian and George Papadopoulos. Their conversation was overheard by another human being who reported it to Steele, or, alternatively, their conversation was recorded on a wire.

Another drunken conversation involving Papadopoulos, this one with the Australian Ambassador to London, Alexander Downer, in which Papadopoulos claims that the Russians have thousands of Clinton emails, was used by the FBI to corroborate Steele's claims about Russian hacking.

Earlier, in 2001, it was another "sexed up" dossier that led to the Iraq War tragedy, that one based on the incredible and unbelievable claims of a hustler, the informant called "Curveball." Analysts in both the CIA and MI6 doubted Curveball's charges concerning Iraq's possession of weapons of mass destruction, but those

George Papadopoulos booking photo after he was arrested by the FBI at Dulles Airport, July 28.

doubts were ignored by an Anglo-American chain of command bent on war. Following the war, both the UK and the U.S.A. finally admitted that Curveball was a con man and that his story, leading to tens of thousands of unnecessary deaths and the birth of ISIS, was all a convenient lie, a hoax—information warfare at its finest.

It is no accident that the man intimately involved in concocting the 2001 sexed-up Iraq dossier, Sir Richard Dearlove, also counseled Christopher Steele regarding Steele's dirty dossier against Donald Trump, according to the *Washington Post*. Dearlove, the former head of Britain's MI6, is portrayed as a mentor to both Christopher Steele and his business partner, Chris Burroughs. The former British Ambassador to Russia, Sir Andrew Wood, is an associate of Steele and Burrows in their London-based firm, Orbis Business Intelligence, Ltd.

This British effort has been portrayed, accurately, as a "full-spectrum [British] information [warfare] operation"[1] aimed at determining the result of the 2016 American election, and, following the election, poisoning the early Trump presidency and setting the stage for Trump's impeachment. Since the techniques for such an operation are well known by spies on both sides of the Atlantic, there is little room to argue that the participating American intelligence personages working with Steele were somehow "duped" by his actions. Everything points to those in contact with Steele as being witting participants in a conspiracy against the United States. This is why the British government is prepared to invoke Britain's "Official Secrets Act" to prevent Christopher Steele from testifying in a libel lawsuit brought against him in London by Alexander Gubarev, and in a similar suit brought against the publication *BuzzFeed* in the United States. The seventeenth Memo of Steele's dirty dossier, published by *BuzzFeed*, falsely accuses Gubarev of conducting cyberattacks

---

1. Peter Van Buren provides an excellent analysis of Steele's information warfare techniques in his Feb. 15, 2018 *American Conservative* article "Christopher Steele: The Real Foreign Influence in the 2016 Election?"

screen grab from the Independent of London

British press coming to the defense of Christopher Steele.

According to a February 11 article by Paul Sperry in *Real Clear Investigations*, the House Intelligence Committee will follow its explosive Nunes Memo detailing FBI and Justice Department's illegalities while pimping Steele's British product to the U.S. FISA Court, with a memo tracing the use of Steele's dirty dossier by the State Department. That will be followed by a memo detailing the relationship of various Obama Administration intelligence officials to the Steele Dossier, including Leon Panetta, Susan Rice, Samantha Power, CIA chief John Brennan, and Director of National Intelligence James Clapper. Sperry, citing a House Intelligence Committee source, notes that the Committee is particularly focused on Brennan, who "did more than anyone to promulgate the dirty dossier" and then lied to Congress about what he knew about it. It is anticipated that this investigation will lead, inexorably, to the center of the conspiracy against Trump which was hatched by the British in collusion with the Obama White House.

As our Mueller Dossier emphasizes, Christopher Steele's dirty dossier is the foundational document for the coup being run against the President. Tracing its use, like a red dye, provides a reasonably complete map of the criminal conspiracy at issue. It leads from MI6 to the Obama White House. It involves the heads of the Obama national security apparatus including the FBI, the CIA, the DNI, the NSA, the Justice Department, the Department of Defense and the State

against the Democratic Party and others on behalf of the Russian government.

Two Senators Continue the Case

Following the release of the "Nunes Memo" Feb. 2, and apoplectic fits over the nation's airways and in its newspapers from those caught up in the British operation, Senators Chuck Grassley and Lindsey Graham secured a less-redacted version of their criminal referral of Christopher Steele to the United States Department of Justice for prosecution, releasing it Feb. 8. The criminal referral provides even more facts about the astonishing fraud on the FISA Court conducted by former Deputy Attorney General Sally Yates, James Comey and others. Senators Graham and Grassley believe that Steele lied to the FBI about his contacts with the media. Lying to the FBI, 18 U.S.C. §1001 False Statements, is the same felony Michael Flynn was charged with.

Senator Chuck Grassley (R-Iowa) on left, and Senator Lindsey Graham (R-S.C.).

Department, and the Russian and Eurasian desks of all of these agencies. It involves practically everyone who ran the coup in Ukraine. It also obviously involves the Hillary Clinton Campaign and those forming her shadow government had she won the election. All of these people intersect British intelligence and Christopher

DoD/R.D. Ward
Leon Panetta

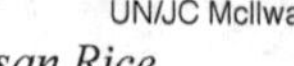

UN/JC McIlwaine
Susan Rice

UN/Manuel Elias
Samantha Power

Steele. All of the activities of British intelligence in the 2016 election need to be put under an investigative microscope. As for the journalists who worked with Steele—they have, for years, had a difficult time demonstrating that they are anything other than paid stenographers and copy editors for a wide variety of intelligence agencies.

In our Mueller dossier, we focus on the motive for this crime, without which the list of names and events now under scrutiny loses its meaning. By their own report, in the *Guardian*, the British war against Donald Trump began in 2014-2015, with concerns about Trump's alleged "softness" on Russia based on years of surveillance of Trump by MI6 and GCHQ. The *Guardian* claims that Robert Hannigan, the former head of GCHQ, was the principal whistleblower concerning an alleged Trump/Russia connection in 2015 based on GCHQ surveillance.

Whether such surveillance actually occurred, or whether the leak to the *Guardian* was designed to provide Christopher Steele's shoddy claims the aura of *gravitas* for information warfare purposes, remains an open question. According to the *Guardian* account, Hannigan personally passed the evidence compiled by the GCHQ on Trump and Russia to CIA Director John Brennan in June 2016. It was then that Brennan launched a "major inter-agency investigation," which included both the FBI and DNI James Clapper.

Steele's first memo was completed June 20, 2016, and his first meeting with an FBI official was July 5, just weeks before Trump received the Republican nomination. Steele, a source for the FBI in Eurasian organized crime investigations and the FIFA (Fédération Internationale de Football Association) criminal prosecution, met with Michael Gaeta, then working for the

White House/Pete Souza
John Brennan

LBJ Library/Jay Godwin
James Clapper

FBI liaison office in Rome. Gaeta and Steele had collaborated previously on Eurasian organized crime investigations. Under FBI procedures, Gaeta became the case agent, overseeing Steele in operations against Trump beginning in September of 2016, operations which the FBI, at least on paper, controlled.

The Recent Weeks' Developments: Big Problems for the Coup

Beginning in December 2017, the seemingly relentless drumbeat of the coup against the President began to slow. First, Justice Department Inspector General Michael Horowitz allowed the publication of text messages exchanged between Peter Strzok, the number two agent in the FBI's Counterintelligence Division in charge of both Russiagate and the Clinton email investigation, and Lisa Page, his mistress, an FBI attorney. Both had served on Robert Mueller's team until the summer of 2017, when the Inspector General briefed Mueller and Deputy Attorney General Rod Rosenstein that text messages exchanged between them revealed bias against Donald Trump.

Horowitz is examining the FBI's handling of the

CSPAN

Clinton email case as well as the actions of former FBI Deputy Director Andrew McCabe. McCabe did not recuse himself from the Clinton email case after his wife had received a campaign contribution in the hundreds of thousands of dollars from Clinton moneybags, then Virginia Governor Terry McAuliffe. McCabe attended the meeting which arranged the contribution and then campaigned for his wife Jill as she sought a seat in the Virginia State Senate, a big problem under the Hatch Act and normal FBI procedures. It is claimed by FBI agents working the Clinton email case that McCabe stalled key steps in the Clinton email investigation. It is widely reported that a briefing from Horowitz about his preliminary findings was the major reason McCabe was abruptly fired from the FBI Jan. 29.

The texts between Strzok and Page reveal a seething anti-Trump bias and speak of an "insurance policy" against Trump emanating from a meeting in Andy McCabe's office. It is widely assumed that the "insurance policy" was the Trump/Russia investigation, although Strzok had previously texted Page that there was "no there, there" with respect to claims that Donald Trump colluded with Russia.

This was followed by revelations that Mueller's lead prosecutor, the ethically challenged Andrew Weissman, had met with reporters to discuss the case against former Trump campaign manager Paul Manafort, well prior to Manafort's indictment. This is hardly the untraceable leaking for which Mueller is famous, and contravenes both Justice Department and ethical rules. As reported in our Mueller dossier, Weissman is famous for inventing new rules for criminal culpability, a practice he used throughout the Enron cases and the Arthur Andersen prosecution resulting in stunning rebukes from federal judges and from the U.S. Supreme Court. Weissman's fawning praise of former Deputy Attorney General Sally Yates for her grandstanding act of "resistance"—her refusal to defend the Trump Administration in court, which is the actual job of the Department of Justice—had also been revealed in December as the result of an FOIA lawsuit.

On Feb. 2, Devin Nunes, the Chair of the House Permanent Select Committee on Intelligence, released his committee's memo regarding the FBI and Department of Justice use of the Steele dossier in surveillance requests to the Foreign Intelligence Surveillance Court regarding Trump volunteer foreign policy advisor Carter Page. On Feb. 6, Senators Grassley and Graham released a redacted version of their referral of Christopher Steele to the Department of Justice for criminal prosecution, providing further details of the shocking FBI/DOJ fraud on the Foreign Intelligence Court.

Christopher Steele: Con-Man *Extraordinaire*

In using the Steele dossier in the first, October 21, 2016 FISA application for surveillance of Page, the FBI/DOJ officials, including James Comey and former Deputy Attorney General Sally Yates, left the fact that Steele's work had been entirely paid for by the Clinton Campaign and the Democratic National Committee to a non-specific footnote referencing some generic "political" origin.

The FBI also attached a *Yahoo News* article by Michael Isikoff to its FISA application concerning Page. The FBI affirmatively told the Court what Steele had apparently told them, that he only shared his work with Fusion GPS and the FBI, *not* the news media. This created the highly misleading impression that Isikoff's article independently validated Steele's allegations, which otherwise were uncorroborated, when, in fact, Isikoff's article was based on a briefing by Steele himself. Moreover, Steele had already briefed the *Washington Post*, the *New York Times*, CNN, and the *New Yorker*, in addition to Isikoff, at the time of the October 21, 2016 initial application to the FISA Court, for surveillance of Carter Page. Steele had also briefed David Corn of *Mother Jones* in October.

According to the Graham/Grassley account, when

Christopher Steele and Michael Isikoff. (Yahoo News photo illustration: photos: Victoria Jones/AP; Gordon Donovan/Yahoo News)

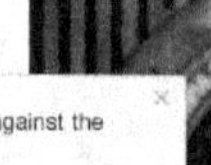

Yahoo news screenshot

Christopher Steele (left) and Michael Isikoff (right).

Corn published his *Mother Jones* article on October 31, it was clear to the FBI that Steele had lied to them about contacts with the news media. His informant status was terminated, but the FBI kept in contact with him through a very high-ranking back channel in the U.S. Department of Justice, Deputy Associate Attorney General Bruce Ohr. Ohr's wife, Nellie Ohr, worked for Steele's U.S. business partner, Fusion GPS, which, with Steele, was heavily funded by the Clinton Campaign and the DNC for opposition research against Donald Trump. Steele confided to Ohr that he would do "anything" to prevent the election of Donald Trump, a fact which the Justice Department never revealed to the FISA court.

When the FBI/DOJ returned to the FISA Court in January 2017 to extend the Page surveillance, it engaged in yet another affirmative misrepresentation to the Court. While disclosing that Steele's informant relationship had been terminated because of his contacts with the news media, the DOJ/FBI claimed to the Court that Steele only talked to the media in anger when the Clinton email investigation was reopened, and the Trump investigation seemed stalled.

As Byron York notes in his <u>ex-cellent analysis</u> for the *Washing-*

cc/MSNBC

Carter Page

ton Examiner, the whole point of the "Chris-was-angry-so-he-talked-to-the-press story was to allow the FBI to claim that Steele's pre-anger work—the dossier—was entirely credible." In the renewal application, the FBI again affirmatively asserted that it did not believe that Steele was the source of Isikoff's Sept. 23 article (which would, of course, call the bona fides of the entire FISA application into question).

Page has claimed publicly that he regularly briefed both the FBI and CIA about his dealings in Russia. According to the FBI, Page was targeted for recruitment by two Russian spies in 2013 who were subsequently prosecuted by the FBI. Page served as an FBI source in that investigation, during which the Russians repeatedly characterized Page as an "idiot" and not worth their time. The FBI cleared Carter Page of any wrongdoing in 2015 concerning the Russian spies. Yet the same FBI, knowing that the Russians considered Page an "idiot" and "not worth their time," asked the Foreign Intelligence Surveillance Court to credit Christopher Steele's absurd assertion that in a deal negotiated by Carter Page, the Russians offered Page and other Trump associates a 19% stake in the state-owned oil company Rosneft, if Trump lifted sanctions against Russia.

While the Democrats argue that Page's prior Russian involvement provides a basis for probable cause, independent of Christopher Steele, for a FISA warrant, the fact that the FBI cleared him in that prior case destroys that claim. The fact that Page has never subsequently been charged or attracted any significant interest from Robert Mueller also should tell you that the whole exercise was for a different purpose—using the fact of the surveillance and investigation to provide credibility for Christopher Steele's black British lies to the news media about Donald Trump. The media reports, in turn, were heavily utilized by the Clinton campaign to discredit Donald Trump.

The Carter Page scandal is only one aspect of FISA abuse by the Obama Administration and the FBI. According to a heavily redacted report from the FISA Court itself, released in April 2017, there were repeated and escalating abuses of FISA by Obama's FBI and Justice Department. In December, Obama and crew substantially loosened the restrictions on receipt of raw surveillance intercepts, providing a cover and a defense to the leakers who attacked the Trump transition.

And Now, the State Department

Nunes, Grassley and Graham have made very clear that the next target of their investigation of the use of the dirty British dossier will be the U.S. State Department. One target already exposed is Jonathan Winer, the Obama State Department's special envoy to Libya. Winer, a long-time number two to John Kerry, dating from Kerry's Senate days, is a significant anti-Putin fanatic who says that he has collaborated with Christopher Steele since 2009-2010, the point at which Steele went into private business in Britain, and the point at which Glenn Simpson founded Fusion GPS and began partnering with Steele here in the United States. Winer, Steele, and Simpson were in the business of selling intelligence—most of which centered on Russia—to private clients.

According to interviews of Steele by British journalist and foreign correspondent for the *Guardian* newspaper, Luke Harding, the lucrative part of this partnership involved providing dirt to competing Russian oligarchs and gangsters in their wars with one another. This, obviously, is a perfect cover for intelligence operations conducted by the British into Russia. This is also why it is such a fatal mistake to pursue the tragic red herring of partisan Republican cries that the "real collaboration" with the Russians occurred via the Clinton campaign because Christopher Steele had a relationship with such as Russian oligarch Oleg Deripaska.

Department of State

John Kerry (left) and Jonathan Winer (right).

The real issue is war and peace, and the British are gambling on a strategy of tension and possible war as the means to maintain their power. The British have been playing this game with Russian oligarchs, who have compromised themselves to the British, financially and otherwise, since before the collapse of the Soviet Union. It is the British, not the Russians, who have diddled the United States.

Christopher Steele, Jonathan Winer, Bruce Ohr, Glenn Simpson, former FBI Deputy Director Andrew McCabe, Lisa Page, Nellie Ohr, Roy Godson, Michael Gaeta, and other figures who have taken the stage as part of Russiagate, have all known each other and worked together for a very long time. This is the result of a long-term intelligence focus on Russia, coalescing in Barack Obama's Transnational Organized Crime initiative focused on Eurasian organized crime. Lisa Page, former Trump Russiagate FBI case agent Peter Stzrok's rabidly biased mistress, advanced her career as a result of the FBI's investigation of Ukrainian oligarch Dmitry Firtash, a major investigation within this initiative. Christopher Steele's previous relationships with the FBI stem from the Eurasian Organized Crime Strike Force and the FBI's investigation of FIFA corruption.

Obama's July 2011 National Security Policy named Transnational Organized Crime (TOC) as a threat to U.S. national security. The Obama Administration forged an alliance with the British to combat this "threat" and opened the funding spigots for projects in this area. Fighting TOC, is, in reality, simply another tool for attacking governments, institutions, and people whom the Anglo-Americans disfavor, rather than a serious effort against drugs, drug money laundering, or terrorism.

Jonathan Winer—who formerly played a leading role in John Kerry's Senate investigations of drug money laundering by the Hong Kong and Shanghai Banking Corporation (HSBC), Edmond Safra's Bank of New York, and the Bank of Credit and Commerce International (BCCI) —has, in his later incarnation, drifted to the British side. Winer is credited with coming up with the idea for the Magnitsky Act sanctions against Putin and Russia for his client, British intelligence operative Bill Browder, who is but one of many City of London operatives responsible for looting Russia following the collapse of the Soviet Union. Browder is a protégé of Edmond Safra.

Browder and Winer have collaborated ever since in a worldwide campaign to extend the Magnitsky sanctions against Putin and Russia as part of the new Cold War. Both Sen. John McCain (R-Ariz.) and Sen. Ben Cardin (D-Md.) were instrumental in this campaign. Both are in the dirty chain of people who have worked with Steele. McCain and McCain Institute director for Human Rights and Democracy, David Kramer, became the cutouts for December 2016 efforts to bring the entire Steele dossier forward into full public view through *BuzzFeed*. Cardin, according to word on the street, became a leak point from the State Department of classified dirty memos against both Russia and Trump, a leak campaign coordinated with Hillary Clinton and the Obama White House.

Glenn Simpson's career has focused on gathering dirt against Putin. But, to illustrate the type of actual master employing him, he was also a critical piece in hedge fund monster Paul Singer's destabilization attack on the government of Argentina.

From 2014-2016, Christopher Steele wrote over 100 memos concerning Russia and Ukraine which were provided to Victoria Nuland, the case officer for the Ukraine coup, and to Winer and Secretary of State John Kerry. Nuland has previously stated that U.S. agencies, all working with the National Endowment for Democracy, spent over $5 billion to organize the Ukraine coup which employed neo-Nazis as military shock troops. On Feb. 11, Nuland appeared pre-emptively on national television to deny any use of the Steele memos by the

Victoria Nuland doling out snacks to violent anti-government protesters in Ukraine, December 2013, with Geoffrey Pyatt.

State Department, because doing so would violate the Hatch Act. However, Winer contradicted the suddenly virtuous Victoria in his account, stating that the memos were circulated by State, including Secretary of State John Kerry in the mix.

In addition, it is claimed that notorious Clinton dirty trickster Cody Shearer fed fabricated dirt on Russia and Trump to Steele through Winer. Steele, in turn, fed it to the FBI, as corroborative of Steele's own feral musings.

Another State Department activity in the coup centers on the infamous June 2016 Trump Tower meeting. That meeting involved Donald Trump, Jr., Paul Manafort, Jared Kushner, and the Russian lawyer Natalia Veselnitskaya. According to the emails setting up the meeting, Veselnitskaya was carrying "dirt" on Hillary Clinton provided directly by the Russian government. In the Mueller dossier, we outlined at some length why this meeting bears all the trappings of a sting operation against the Trump campaign in pursuit of corroboration for the Steele dossier's claims.

Veselnitskaya traveled to the United States on a highly unusual State Department business visa issued over the objections of the Justice Department. Robert Otto, the top U.S. intelligence guy on Russia, according to *Foreign Policy* magazine, works at the State Department's Bureau of Intelligence and Research. Otto's emails were hacked and posted on the Internet. They show surveillance of Veselnitskaya's house in Russia prior to her visit to Trump Tower. She claims her children had been threatened. The strange circumstances of this Russian lawyer's visa, the surveillance of her house, and her story about threats, suggest that she was under the control of Washington operatives with respect to the Trump Tower affair. Additional Otto emails show Otto working with David Kramer, former State Department coordinator for Project Democracy and the aide to John McCain, who many believe leaked the Steele Memo to *BuzzFeed*.

FBI raids LaRouche publishing offices, Oct. 7, 1986.

Finally, there are the three Chalupa sisters: Irene at the State Department's Radio Free Europe, Radio Liberty; Arlene, the social media maven in the Ukraine coup; and Alexandra, who coordinated the Clinton Campaign's work with Kiev's intelligence agencies targeting Donald Trump and Paul Manafort. Alexandra claims to have been hacked directly by the Russians while working at the DNC for Clinton because of her research on Paul Manafort. She coordinated her Manafort work with none other than Yahoo's Michael Isikoff.

How Does All This Affect Mueller?

I have characterized Robert Mueller as a modern day Grand Inquisitor, a Torquemada, and a Captain Ahab. But one thing is certain: Strait-laced Bobby Three Sticks, the font of prosecutorial rectitude portrayed by Washington D.C.'s public relations gurus, he most certainly is not. All of the names I have called him reference a ruthless amorality in service of those who have asked him to go to war for them, including the Bush family and other scions of the Anglo-American elite. As detailed in our Mueller Report, our experience with him is up close and personal. Mueller led the immoral, corrupt, and lawless prosecution of Lyndon LaRouche, in which the British and their American satraps called for LaRouche's head on strategic and political policy grounds. As with Donald Trump, they framed LaRouche as a crazy Russian dupe. As with Trump, the primary weapon against LaRouche was an information warfare campaign, endlessly and relentlessly cycling fake news. And, as in the current targeting of President Trump, the British hand was all over the prosecution of LaRouche.

A classified letter from the British government to the FBI in 1982 demanded LaRouche's head. An FBI investigation was launched under Executive Order 12333, in collaboration with the CIA, with full use of the nation's counterintelligence authorities, including surveillance, infiltration, and black propaganda conducted through the news media. A media salon of propagandists from major publications working under the auspices of the Bush family, James Jesus Angleton, and CIA active measures operatives John Train and Walter Raymond, was assembled and pumped out a barrage of salacious lies about LaRouche over a two year period. This "weaponized" information warfare and media campaign was designed to set the stage for a "solution" to the LaRouche problem by either assassination or prosecution. That solution became operative Oct. 6, 1986, with a 400-person raid, under Robert Mueller's direction, on the place where LaRouche was staying and the Leesburg, Virginia offices occupied by LaRouche's associates. The assassination gambit failed, so Mueller prosecuted LaRouche in Boston for obstruction of justice. True to type, however, Mueller's Boston prosecution of LaRouche collapsed in 1988 amid judicial findings of "systemic and institutional prosecutorial misconduct."

The same lack of a moral compass and complete infidelity to the U.S. Constitution resulted in Mueller's coverup of the British/Saudi murder of 3,000 Americans September 11, 2001, his coverup of the depredations of such drug and terrorist financing fronts as BCCI and Banca Nazionale de Lavoro (BNL), his coverup of the cocaine financing of the Bush Administration's adventures in Central America, accomplished by pinning it all on Panama President Manuel Noriega, and his brutal prosecutions of other innocents like former biodefense researcher for the U.S. Army Dr. Steven Hatfill. Mueller bears much responsibility for the unconstitutional surveillance police state under which Americans have lived since September 11, 2001. We detail all of this in our original the Mueller dossier.

As many have pointed out, Mueller has multiple conflicts of interest. He was considered a mentor by the chief witness in his obstruction investigation, James Comey. He ran the FBI for years and has repeatedly stated that he will not countenance criticism of the Bureau. The man in the Department of Justice ultimately responsible for vetting Christopher Steele, John Carlin, is Robert Mueller's former Chief of Staff.[2]

Alan Dershowitz and Andrew McCarthy have argued, persuasively, that Mueller's investigation violates the Constitution and that Rod Rosenstein's letter appointing him was *ultra vires*, that is, lacking in legal authority.

Under Article II, Sec. 2.2 of the U.S. Constitution, the President controls the Department of Justice, like

World Trade Center twin towers under attack in New York City, Sept. 11, 2001.

it or not. The remedy for an abuse of the President's authority is in an election, not turning the Justice Department into some sort of independent star chamber bereft of control. Moreover, independent counsels are appointed to investigate crimes, not allegations of collusion, which is a counterintelligence and national security function. The President has the authority under the Constitution to oversee all counterintelligence investigations and to fire anyone or to end their operations as he deems necessary. It is not only an authority, it is an obligation of the President of the United States.

Further, Rod Rosenstein's grant of authority to Mueller in his appointment letter to investigate "any other crimes" he discovers in the course of his counterintelligence investigation is a *de facto* hunting license, which Congress sought to prevent when it refused to renew the Independent Counsel statute. The regulations under which Mueller is operating dictate that he is to investigate specific crimes where the Department of Justice is shown to have a conflict of interest.

This does not mean that Mueller should be "fired" by the President in any of the crazed scenarios floated by the moral and intellectual dead heads presently constituting the leadership of the formerly great party of Franklin Roosevelt and John F. Kennedy. It means that the Congress—and others with access to the classified

---

2. See Scott Ritter's extremely useful Feb. 4, 2018 review of the Carter Page FISA scandal and Christopher Steele's relationship to the FBI, "The Ugly Truth in the Nunes Memo."

Philip Mudd, former CIA officer.

documents and subpoena power—should pursue each of the stages of the criminal conspiracy against Donald Trump outlined in our Mueller dossier. The truth, finally exposed, will leave Mueller with nothing to investigate or prosecute. The truth, finally exposed, will put the actual criminals, like Christopher Steele, in the dock, as requested by Senators Grassley and Graham.

Cornered, Snarling Dogs

With the story of Russiagate falling apart, defenders of the FBI and CIA are resorting to blatant threats against the President. Philip Mudd, a former CIA officer whom Robert Mueller personally moved to the FBI to supervise Mueller's huge informant program, told CNN in August 2017 that "this government is going to kill this guy," referring to Trump. On Feb. 2, Mudd, now a CNN consultant, lashed out against the Nunes memo on CNN. Parroting the line of Congressional Democrats about the memo, he said it is an attack on the FBI's "ability to conduct an investigation with integrity.... The FBI people are ticked.... You think you can intimidate the director? You better think again, Mr. President." He added, "I know how the game is played. We're going to win."

The media has gone out seeking reinforcements, as the pubic continues to reject Russiagate as a myth and a hoax. CNN just hired Josh Campbell, a former top aide to Comey, to join its team, while NBC television hired John Brennan to provide "commentary."

Additionally, there is Laurence Tribe, Barack Obama's Harvard law professor and a formerly respected Constitutional scholar. Tribe's inner alien has been running loose ever since he succumbed to Trump derangement syndrome in November 2016. Now he has sallied forth to claim, on the pages of the *New York Times*, that Devin Nunes and other members of Congress are guilty of obstruction of justice because they undermined Robert Mueller's phony investigation. As President Trump quipped, if you fight back, you are obstructing, in the opinion of those who have criminalized political debate.

What you are really hearing in the protests against Nunes and Grassley and against the unraveling of the Russiagate charade are the snarls of people who have been caught and are about to have to face the music. They can't stop themselves because they are too exposed. In a Fox Television interview, Devin Nunes spoke of the serenity which comes from knowing that the facts and the law are on your side and about watching how cartoonish and comical those caught by you react to being exposed. The would-be emperors truly have no clothes.

But, the danger remains and will intensify. After all, a shift in the way the world has been run since the death of Franklin Roosevelt is at stake. Our so-called intelligence gurus rave about dictatorships while they surveil everyone and seek wholesale censorship of social media and news publications so that only one viewpoint impregnates the American mind. The Truth Ministry of George Orwell was fully implemented under George Bush and Barack Obama. The disclosures of recent weeks and the trail left by Christopher Steele create the potential for a real challenge to the London/Washington "narrative," a real potential to drain the swamp.

As Devin Nunes said, we can win this fight because the facts and the truth are on our side. We can win this fight now, but we need you to join it. If you haven't read the full Mueller dossier, please do so. While you are at it, read and endorse LaRouche PAC's 2018 electoral platform, which can bring true prosperity back to our country. How to create such, I guarantee you, the British agents and coup participants do not have a clue. That is, ultimately, their fatal flaw. As the Chinese would say, they have lost the mandate of heaven.

REPORT FROM GERMANY

Instead of Geopolitics, A Vision and a Framework for Peace in the 21st Century!

by Helga Zepp-LaRouche, chairwoman of the German political party, Civil Rights Movement Solidarity (BüSo)

Feb. 16—It is not just Germany's Social Democratic Party (SPD) which is in the deepest crisis of its history. It is the entire, old paradigm of the West, based on geopolitics, neoliberal financial and economic policies, and democracy—which, on closer inspection, is not all that democratic. That the protagonists of this obsolete world view lack any idea for a positive future, has just been made clear in the continuing drama around the negotiations for a Grand Coalition in Germany—Martin Schulz, Sigmar Gabriel, Andrea Nahles, and the CDU. Not a word is uttered on the existential questions, such as the safeguarding of world peace, or a solution to avert the renewed threat of financial collapse, or the overcoming of poverty in Europe—there is only indecent haggling over party positions. This is crystal clear to everyone.

Obviously, these Grand Coalition politicians are just as incapable as Hillary Clinton of questioning the reasons for their political failure; not even its collapse to 16% in the polls can wake up the SPD. And for Ms. Merkel, she seems to believe the world is one will and representation:[1] when she repeats—completely oblivi-

Wolfgang Ischinger (left), Chairman of the Munich Security Conference, interviewed by Christoph Heinemann.

1. Arthur Schopenhauer's work, *The World as Will and Representation* (*Die Welt als Wille und Vorstellung*), argues that we perceive the world "in the theater of our own mind."

ous to reality—that of course she will form a stable government.

Geopolitics and Arrogance

But it is not only the politicians who twist the truth. There is also the method of fallacy of composition—manipulating the context of a discussion by inserting or omitting a portion of the truth in such a way as to lead the reader or listener to the wrong conclusion. On February 15, on the eve of the Munich Security Conference, conference chairman Wolfgang Ischinger, in an interview on *Deutschlandfunk* with Christoph Heinemann, provided a classic example of how to pervert the truth. He said there was a high risk of a military confrontation between major powers, because of the profound mistrust between Moscow and Washington.

Xinhua/Ma Zhancheng

China President Xi Jinping.

The true part of this statement is the high risk of war between the United States and Russia. What Ischinger does not mention, however, is that Trump has sought and still strives for an improvement in relations with Russia, and precisely for this reason the Obama administration's secret service chiefs, in collaboration with the British intelligence service MI6, launched a coup attempt against him with the alleged "Russiagate" story. That attempted coup was blown wide open in the course of Congressional investigations over the past weeks, and criminal investigations are underway against the putschists.

Indicative of the side that Ischinger has taken is the theme of the Munich conference: "To the brink—and back?" where the "brink" does not mean the imminent danger of war, but rather the shock of Trump's election victory as "the new figure in Washington," one year ago. But fortunately, Ischinger went on, there are reassuring signs now, the U.S. troops are still in Europe, and the most radical innovators are no longer in the administration.

Christoph Heinemann used the same fallacy of composition method by asking Ischinger if the international community is responding adequately to Chinese hegemony; he thus insinuates propitiatingly that China is seeking hegemony, whereas Chinese politicians have put just the opposite on the agenda with their offer of win-win cooperation. Ischinger, in his answer, omits to say that it is not China's alleged efforts that are dividing the EU, but rather the fact that the EU has done absolutely nothing for the eastern and central European states, while China is building infrastructure there, which is what makes cooperation with China so attractive. When Heinemann asks, in view of the emergence of prosperity in record time in China, whether democracy, the rule of law, and freedom are not as imperative as the West always says, Ischinger essentially repeats this assertion, saying it is only a matter of time before the Chinese turn to democracy.

Who Cares About Poverty?

It would be a tragedy for Germany and the world if we are unable to free ourselves from this geopolitical and highly arrogant thinking. It is an indisputable fact that China has not only freed 700 million people from poverty, but is currently conducting an unprecedented campaign to free the last remaining 30 million people still living in poverty and help them achieve a good standard of living by building infrastructure in poor regions, with education, job creation, and the rest. China is extending this experience to developing countries, and that is why cooperation with the New Silk Road is so attractive. The overcoming of poverty is obviously not only the byproduct of economic growth, but rather the conscious policy of the Chinese government. In Germany, there is also economic growth, but one out of every six children here is poor.

The geopoliticians of the West are obviously furious at the unstoppable economic rise of China, which is, after all, a nation of 1.4 billion people with a 5,000-year-old continuous culture that had been at the forefront of technological development for many centuries. Xi Jinping gave an absolutely visionary report at the 19th National Congress of the Communist Party, which is now also available in German and should be read by anyone who wants to form his or her own opinion. After Xi laid out the perspectives for the development of China by 2050, and announced that China would assume greater responsibility on the international stage, it took three months for the various geopolitical think tanks to work out their counter-attack. From the Australian secret service to the American think tanks CSIS and CFR, to the Soros-funded ECFR and the German think tank MERICS, an obviously coordinated attack on China's New Silk Road policy as an alleged imperial strategy has been launched.

Western 'Democracy' As a Weapon

Clearly, China is no longer prepared to accept these attacks

Ancient Chinese philosopher Mencius.

without comment, attacks that project the geopolitical thinking of their authors. In an article dated February 11, 2018, the *Global Times* countered by describing in detail the method of regime change that hides behind the facade of democracy. The West claims a monopoly on democracy, but this does not correspond to reality, according to author Thomas Hon Wing Polin. The Chinese term "minzhu" literally means "the people are in charge," which is the essence of democracy, he points out. But the Western liberal form of democracy "neither puts the people in charge, nor does it put their interests uppermost." In reality, it is an oligarchy "that serves the interests of a tiny minority at the expense of the vast majority." On the other hand, Mencius, in the 4th Century B.C., defended the people's right to remove their government if it does not fulfill its task, and to this day there is no greater disaster for China's leaders, than in forfeiting the "mandate of heaven." In the sense of putting the people's interest first, "China is already more democratic than the West," he says.

But, he continues, the Western concept of democracy, on the contrary, is a weapon of the Western imperium for perpetual world domination, a voodoo spell that "turns the brains of otherwise intelligent people into mush." It is possible that democracies actually function domestically, but in foreign policy they represent hegemony, neo-colonialism, and dictatorship. The next time someone praises democracy as the best model of government, keep this in mind, the author advises.

Even though the political establishment in Germany is far from realizing it, the old paradigm of geopolitics and neoliberal economic policy has long been floundering. However, there is a way out of the current dilemma: The coup attempt against President Trump can become a boomerang for those who instigated it, and the "Four Laws" put forward by my husband Lyndon LaRouche can prevail in the United States: the Glass-Steagall banking separation law, a credit system in the tradition of Alexander Hamilton, massive investment in building modern infrastructure, and the launching of a nuclear fusion program and space exploration—and the United States accepting Xi Jinping's offer to cooperate with the New Silk Road.

In Germany, external intervention is obviously needed, as the political minds in this country have fallen prey to partisan carnage and jockeying for positions. But the BüSo stands for the new paradigm: The New Silk Road will become the worldwide bridge of understanding of all nations and cultures of this world, beyond the antiquated geopolitics that have already brought us two world wars.

zepp-larouche@eir.de

Growing Neocon China Hysteria Shows Silk Road Spirit Is Unstoppable

This is an edited transcript of the Feb. 15, 2018 Schiller Institute New Paradigm Webcast, with Helga Zepp-LaRouche.

Harley Schlanger: Hello. I'm Harley Schlanger with the Schiller Institute. I'd like to welcome you to this week's webcast with the Schiller Institute Founder and President Helga Zepp-LaRouche.

Helga, I think what we need to start with this week, is the issue of geopolitics. You've always emphasized that geopolitics is an imperial game, it's part of the old paradigm and the greatest threat to mankind. This was on display yesterday in the U.S. Senate: The Intelligence Committee had the Threat Assessment hearing; Dan Coats, the Director of National Intelligence, said, "Frankly the United States is under attack." Senator Marco Rubio (R-Fla) said, "China is the biggest threat." He said, "it's aggressively promoting infrastructure as part of its long geopolitical arm."

What's behind this?

Helga Zepp-LaRouche: As it becomes clear that China will become, sooner or later, the largest economy in the world—it's already bypassing the United States in certain respects—there is an hysterical response from those people in the West who are holding to the concep-

tion of a unipolar world, the idea of a *Pax Americana*, where the United States is the only dominating superpower. China is a nation of 1.4 billion people that will eventually become stronger. especially with the kind of science- and technology-oriented policy that China is pursuing. It is clear that some people are responding to that with the idea that they must contain China.

Now, I think it should be clear to anybody that that is a complete impossibility, unless you go to war.

China has answered the recent attacks—which come from Australia, from the United States, and from certain European think tanks—in a very calm way. For example, there was a response to the claim that China is a "competitor" or a "rival," as Trump said in his State of the Union Address. There was a quite reasonable article in *Global Times*, answering this, making the point that the United States has to make an historic choice. Clearly, the rise of China has caused certain strategic phobias among certain people, who have recognized that China is offering a different development model which is especially attractive to developing countries. Some people are now reacting to that. However, cooperation is the only way for these two largest countries in the world—the United States and China—to find a pathway leading to collaboration; then they have a bright future.

It is completely crazy to say that everything China

C-Span

Senator Marco Rubio: "China is the biggest threat."

C-Span

Dan Coats, Director of National Intelligence: "The United States is under attack."

does—the Chinese culture, the Chinese system—that all of this is a threat to the West. That is absolutely not the case, and China has offered cooperation. Anything else will only lead to catastrophe.

There is, however, a big difference in how President Trump is acting; while all of these attacks were going on, he met with State Councillor Yang Jiechi in Washington, and they reopened the four-level strategic dialogues, which will continue. I think this is very good. But, the propaganda campaign against China right now is reaching an absolutely unprecedented furor.

Schlanger: At the same time, we're seeing the changes going on with Russiagate; you hear very little these days about questions of what Russia did, and what Trump did. But there are new things emerging. I think it's quite interesting: The Obama role is starting to be talked about. Joe diGenova had another statement. What's your assessment of what's going on with the whole Russiagate story?

Zepp-LaRouche: I think what Joseph diGenova points out, which I think is quite relevant, is that the counter-memo to the Nunes memorandum, coming from Rep. Adam Schiff (D-Calif), was kept back by the FBI and the DOJ because there are certain statements in it which needed to be redacted according to these two institutions. DiGenova points to the fact that the statement—because there is a criminal investigation going on—is very interesting. He says that all the culprits who were involved in this Russiagate coup attempt eventually will face criminal prosecution. So that's one thing.

The role of former President Obama is now an issue. There was an odd email which Susan Rice sent as a memo to herself on Jan. 20, 2017, in which she reported a meeting involving Obama, Biden, Comey, and herself. That meeting was held to ensure that matters relating to Russia not be passed on by the intelligence services to incoming President Trump because of the suspicion of his collusion with Russia. Now, that's quite incredible, that the outgoing President would instruct the intelligence services to withhold information from an incoming President. This refers to a meeting which apparently took place on Jan. 5, and then one day later, the four heads of the intelligence services went to Trump in the Trump Tower—this was still in the transition period—and they told him about the supposed collusion with Russia. Later, when Comey testified for over two hours before the Senate Intelligence Committee, he admitted this was his "J. Edgar Hoover moment."

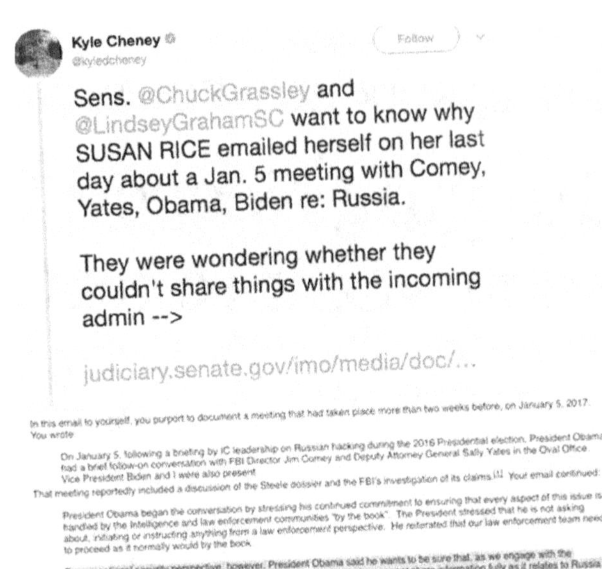

In this email to yourself, you purport to document a meeting that had taken place more than two weeks before, on January 5, 2017. You wrote:

> On January 5, following a briefing by IC leadership on Russian hacking during the 2016 Presidential election, President Obama had a brief follow-on conversation with FBI Director Jim Comey and Deputy Attorney General Sally Yates in the Oval Office. Vice President Biden and I were also present.

That meeting reportedly included a discussion of the Steele dossier and the FBI's investigation of its claims.[1] Your email continued:

> President Obama began the conversation by stressing his continued commitment to ensuring that every aspect of this issue is handled by the Intelligence and law enforcement communities "by the book". The President stressed that he is not asking about, initiating or instructing anything from a law enforcement perspective. He reiterated that our law enforcement team needs to proceed as it normally would by the book.
>
> From a national security perspective, however, President Obama said he wants to be sure that, as we engage with the incoming team, we are mindful to ascertain if there is any reason that we cannot share information fully as it relates to Russia.

The next part of your email remains classified. After that, you wrote:

> The President asked Comey to inform him if anything changes in the next few weeks that should affect how we share classified information with the incoming team. Comey said he would.

This is all now in the public domain. Everything we said in the dossier on Mueller *"Robert Mueller Is an Amoral Legal Assassin; He Will Do His Job If You Let Him!"* which we published last September, is now proven to be absolutely on point by these congressional investigations. The battle for where the United States will go looks much better for Trump than for the people who are attempting the coup against him.

Schlanger: To go back to what you said about the Susan Rice memo: if you look at the Intelligence Committee hearing yesterday, it seems as though the heads of intelligence today are still holding to the same line that they did under Obama.

Zepp-LaRouche: Yes, they keep saying it, but that doesn't mean that these investigations in the House and Senate will cease. Some mills are milling slowly, but they're milling.

Schlanger: The other big news from the United States was the introduction of the White House infrastructure proposal. What's your assessment on that? It doesn't seem to be what it was cracked up to be.

Zepp-LaRouche: I think it's noted as a good thing by many people that there is, finally, somebody proposing an infrastructure program, because infrastructure is a phenomenon which lasts 30, 40, 50 years, or maybe sometimes even longer. But eventually it ages. It disintegrates and that's what we see in many places in the United States—the roads, the nonexisting high-speed system, the general condition of bridges and so forth. So it's a good thing that it is being discussed.

But I think that the way Trump unveiled it, with the hope there will be private investors, with a lot of burdens falling on state and local governments, will not succeed. China has noted that point in commenting that the political system in the United States is making it impossible, because the moment Trump said anything about his program, the Democrats completely opposed it. Obviously infrastructure is in the national interest, and therefore should be a nonpartisan issue. But the fact that you have this partisan system in the United States and elsewhere in the West, as part of the so-called "democratic" system, prevents any progress in this respect. Therefore, it's all the more important that a professor from Beijing University presented the idea of investing the large foreign exchange reserves which China has, especially in the form of U.S. Treasuries, in infrastructure in the United States.

This is a proposal which we made early on because China has the financing and China has the infrastructure expertise. They have built an enormous amount of high-speed train systems and other infrastructure. So I think that that would be the only way to make this function. In addition, you need Glass-Steagall, you need a National Bank in the tradition of Alexander Hamilton, and a credit system, and then the cooperation with the Belt and Road Initiative; and then it would function.

So that remains the task. In the United States, our colleagues are encouraging state legislators and others to bring pressure from the base, to overcome both neocon pressure in the Republican Party and the Democratic opposition to Trump's infrastructure promises, through a program in the national interests of the United States, which would also be a peace-building measure. That is the battle right now.

Schlanger: We also have this fairly interesting article in Bloomberg about the Chinese economy, where they say, our models show that it should have crashed, but it hasn't crashed. They say they're confounded by this. It's obvious, these models don't work, but the Chinese are aware of that, aren't they?

Zepp-LaRouche: Yes. As a matter of fact, as these attacks against China have escalated, China had a very interesting counterattack on the Western trumpeting of democracy, saying that democracy is the hobby-horse of many people in the West, but in reality, it is not being practiced in the common interest, but it's basically being used as a weapon to defend the interest of an oligarchy. The West cannot make the sole claim of having democratic systems. The Chinese say that their system goes back to the ancient Chinese philosopher Mencius, who demanded that government must follow the Mandate of Heaven. In China it is the highest obligation of the party to follow the Mandate of Heaven, which means the common good of the people.

The Chinese say, in their counterattack, that democracy is being used for regime change, and that when the West targets a country, people are incited to agitate for so-called democracy. Then the Western mainstream media plays up street demonstrations. If everything goes according to plan it leads to regime change. If it

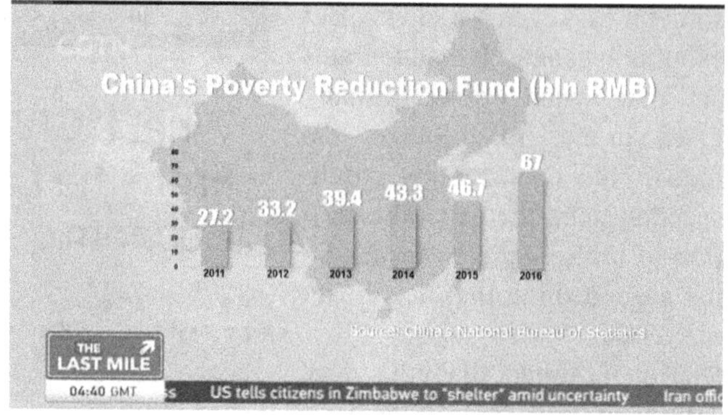

CGTN

doesn't go well, the next step is a violent color revolution.

These renewed, sharp responses coming from China reflect the fact that they are not at all intimidated. They're quite aware of the double standard of the so-called "liberal system" which claims to be liberal, but instead demands global hegemony and top-down global control of the rules. This double standard is visible for anybody who wants to see it.

There is a new tone of self-confidence and self-assuredness in the Chinese responses to these accusations.

Schlanger: And I would assume the Chinese have to be asking the question, "What's wrong with reducing poverty?" And here we see this situation where poverty is growing in the West, it has been growing from the 2001 period on, and yet, Chinese efforts to alleviate poverty, not just in China, but also in their neighboring countries and all around the world as well, is seen as somehow an imperial, expansionist policy.

I mean—do the Chinese have a reaction to that?

Zepp-LaRouche: They have an impressive program to alleviate poverty inside China by 2020. For those people who are interested, there is a documentary on CGTN, the Chinese Global Television Network, where they show how every spot is mapped out, every village where you have poverty. The government has mapped out every family's situation, to find out what has to be done to overcome that poverty—be it education, infrastructure, industrialization, relocation of people to better-off areas—and President Xi Jinping is very much hands-on. He travels to some villages, not

Xinhua/Lan Hongguang

China's President Xi Jinping, overseeing China's poverty reduction program, talks to villagers in China's northeast province of Heilongjiang.

all of them, but some. He talks to the families, he makes it clear that it is his personal concern that the goal of eliminating poverty by 2020 is reached. This is very, very impressive.

There was another article in the Chinese press, which reports that infrastructure development and poverty alleviation are also areas of competition. Not only is the economic growth of China absolutely incredible and outstanding, but so is the infrastructure building and poverty alleviation.

The West must suffer being judged: Who is doing more for their people? Is it China, or is it the West, with their so-called austerity systems? If you look at Europe, there is now a new study out by the European Center for Economic Research, which looked at the difference, after the 2008 crisis, between those countries which had an anti-cyclical focus on basic research and development, R&D, and had a massive increase in productivity—the countries that did that were Germany, Denmark, Sweden, and Finland—as compared to those countries which were hit by EU Troika austerity policy—Greece, Italy, Spain, Portugal, Poland, Czech Republic, and Lithuania—which had to make deep cuts also in basic research and development, which resulted in a terrible collapse in productivity.

I think there is something fundamentally wrong with the system of the free market, which after all is not that free, given the fact that all central banks do is bail out the banks by pumping money for the benefit of the speculators. The rich become richer, and the poor become more poor, and the middle class is shrinking.

Wilhelm von Kardorff

This article posted by Bloomberg which you referenced earlier, is very interesting, because the author admits that according to his theory, China should be collapsing. It should have meager economic growth, but obviously the contrary is the case. He says that China is doing everything that, according to his theory, is terrible, like state intervention, party control—things like that—and China is prospering. And actually, he says, he's not yet ready to completely overturn his theory, but he's willing to make corrections.

To foster such corrections, we need a public debate. What are the economic criteria for a functioning economy? Let us present the works of my husband, Lyndon LaRouche, and his development of physical economy, going back to Leibniz, to Friedrich List, to Henry C. Carey, to Wilhelm von Kardorff—who was the economic advisor of Bismarck and was one of the key influences in bringing about the industrial revolution in Germany—and compare those approaches to the so-called free market model. I think we have to have a real debate. What is the cause of wealth? Is it money, or is it the idea of the creativity of the individual, which then leads to scientific and technological discoveries, which applied in the production process leads to an increase in productivity, which then leads to more wealth, longevity, and all of these things?

We need a discussion about that. The notion of what is economy, equating that with money, has really become one of the axiomatic assumptions of a failing system. So we need a debate about that.

Schlanger: One of the great contributions of your

German Chancellor Otto von Bismarck.

husband was to make the connection between geopolitical doctrine as an imperial doctrine, and the imposition of these kinds of economic policies, which only work for the handful of the most wealthy.

The focus of the Schiller Institute has been to extend the Silk Road into the World Land-Bridge. We're seeing that now with the bioceanic railway, the progress in Africa. What can you tell us about how these projects are advancing?

Zepp-LaRouche: They're developing very well: There was just a confirmation from the Chinese Embassy in Brazil, that the bioceanic railway, connecting the Pacific and the Atlantic from Brazil to Peru, is still very much on the agenda. A feasibility study has been made. This is on a good trajectory as are all the projects agreed upon at the China-CELAC meeting—the Caribbean and Latin American countries meeting with China. The Africa projects are also all progressing very well. The World Land-Bridge is becoming a reality, very quickly, to the benefit of all countries that are participating in it.

Schlanger: I'd like to come back, as we wrap this up, to the question of geopolitics. We got a question from a viewer, who wants to know why you always blame British geopolitical manipulations for World War I and World War II? And they ask the question, what did they do, and what were they responding to?

Why don't you give us the answer to that?

Zepp-LaRouche: If you look at the British Empire's policy toward the European Continent in the 19th Century, they clearly were extremely upset about the industrial revolution in Germany, introduced by Bismarck. Bismarck, as I mentioned earlier, had initially been a free-trade advocate, working with Prussian Junkers. But then he became acquainted with the theories of Henry C. Carey through his friend, Wilhelm von Kardorff, who was the head of the German business association at the time. They recognized the fundamental difference between what Friedrich List had called the "American System," and the British free-trade system.

Bismarck became a proponent of protectionism. This led to a very quick industrial revolution in Germany. The British, through their royal relatives, manipulated the ouster of Bismarck, which was really a tragedy. Bismarck was quite smart and had strategically established a peace order on the European Continent, through diplomatic treaties with every nation. With Russia, he had the secret Reinsurance Treaty, which was negotiated to prevent a possible outbreak of war, if French-German tensions were to develop.

His successors were not so smart. They didn't pay attention to this Reinsurance Treaty with Russia. The British began to manipulate the chessboard of the European countries, step by step, creating incidents to establish the Entente Cordiale; the Triple Entente; the war between Russia and Japan; and the Balkan Wars. Soon every country was set, and ready to go. The shooting in Sarajevo was only the trigger but not the cause for World War I.

Behind that was the idea of geopolitics as it had been developed by Mackinder, Milner, and later by Haushofer, which was the crazy idea that whoever controls the Eurasian land-mass will control the world, to the disadvantage of the Atlantic rim countries—the United States and England. That idea of orchestrating conflict to prevent such a development, became a live issue with the building of the Trans-Siberian Railroad in the 1890s. The plans to build a Berlin-Baghdad Rail-

President Franklin Roosevelt, inspecting the construction of the Boulder Dam, Sept. 30, 1935.

way, was regarded by the British at that time, as a fundamental threat to their control of the sea trade.

Now, obviously, today, with the New Silk Road, if you think in terms of geopolitics, you could easily arrive at the same mistaken conclusion, and I think that is the British thinking. And as we can see now, in the case of Sen. Marco Rubio, or the intelligence heads of the United States, that is their thinking.

But as I have said, many, many times, geopolitics had led to essentially all the wars in history. It led to two World Wars. Those who had read *Mein Kampf* and knew the background of Hitler, knew that eventually a war between Russia and Germany would result. There were financial backers who wanted Hitler to come to power—Bank of England Governor Montagu Norman, the Harriman interests in the United States, and others. This situation leading to World War II was manipulated; it was clear it would result in such a war.

It should be clear to everybody who has not lost his marbles, that in the age of thermonuclear weapons, you cannot continue this game, without risking the extinction of civilization! And I think what China has proposed with its "win-win cooperation," with its offers of China-United States cooperation on the basis of new relations among major powers, the offer for European countries to cooperate—that is catapulting humanity to a higher level of cooperation and reason! And I think it is so much in our self-interest.

What is the problem with the United States? It's not that China is rising, the problem is that the United States has moved away from the policies of the Founding Fathers, of Lincoln, of Franklin D. Roosevelt, of Kennedy. The United States, indeed, could become great again, by returning to those policies, and then the U.S.A. would not regard China as a threat. It's only when the West is collapsing that there is agitation to portray the rising power as a threat. But as Chinese ambassador to Washington Cui Tiankai said—and I think that that is definitely something to think about—that in history there were 16 cases where one nation was rising and the then dominant nation was faced with such a situation: In twelve cases, there had been war, and in four cases, the rising country had bypassed the old, dominant one, and itself became the new dominant nation. The Chinese ambassador added: China does not want the twelve cases where it led to war, but it also doesn't want to repeat the four cases, with China taking over and become the unipolar, dominant country. China wants to have respect for the sovereignty of each nation. That is what all the developing countries that are participating in the Belt and Road Initiative are experiencing. That's why they cooperate, they have benefits from it, and they have now, for the first time, the chance to overcome their underdevelopment and poverty.

I think it would be absolutely dangerous to listen to these people who are now saying that everything China represents is a threat. If you look at China, it's actually a very well-functioning economic model: The people are happy, the philosophy is for the common good, and it is not a threat. And I want to keep insisting on that, because nothing could be more dangerous than permitting complete anti-China hysteria and anti-Russia hysteria. And the only consequence of that would be a terrible catastrophe for all of us.

Schlanger: I think from what you just said, it becomes increasingly clear for people, why Donald Trump's desire to have good relations with Russia and China is seen as such a threat to the City of London, and its extended worldwide interests.

Helga, that brings us to the end of the program today. We'll see you next week!

Zepp-LaRouche: Yes, till next week.

The New Silk Road Becomes the World Land-Bridge

The BRICS countries have a strategy to prevent war and economic catastrophe. It's time for the rest of the world to join!

This 374-page report is a road-map to the New World Economic Order that Lyndon and Helga LaRouche have championed for over 20 years.

Includes:

Introduction by Helga Zepp-LaRouche, "The New Silk Road Leads to the Future of Mankind!"

The metrics of progress, with emphasis on the scientific principles required for survival of mankind: nuclear power and desalination; the fusion power economy; solving the water crisis.

The three keystone nations: China, the core nation of the New Silk Road; Russia's mission in North Central Eurasia and the Arctic; India prepares to take on its legacy of leadership.

Other regions: The potential contributions of Southwest, Central, and Southeast Asia, Australia, Europe, and Africa.

The report is available in PDF $35
and in hard copy $50 (softcover) $75 (hardcover)
plus shipping and handling.
Order from http://store.larouchepub.com

WHY CHOOSE SLAVERY?

Frederick Douglass and America as a Principle

by Dennis Speed

Feb. 19—Once again, as with the recent case of liar "Little Dickie" Durbin's "Trump said it, and I heard it!" Haiti whopper, Americans are being intentionally deflected by their national Fake News media from overturning the coup against the Presidency of the United States. As one saying has it, "whenever the media is pushing a big story, find the story they are trying to distract you from." The Mueller "devastating indictment" of thirteen Russians who will never stand trial, itself based on a three-year-old story that has nothing to do with the Presidency, is distracting from the now increasingly abundant evidence that nearly everyone in the Mueller investigative team is being revealed to be—where they are not shown to be directly guilty of high crimes against the Constitution—at least criminally incompetent.

This is evidenced by the FBI's nonfeasance with respect to Florida's Parkland High School mass shooting. Governor Scott of Florida, sensing the mood of white-hot rage building among the parents of the victims and the state's citizenry as a whole, correctly called for the resignation of FBI Director Christopher Wray, whose agency appears to be too busy protecting criminals in its midst, now shown to be working on behalf of British and "American Tory" interests against the President, to protect the American people through even the most rudimentary police work.

National Archives/George K. Warren
Frederick Douglass, ca. 1879.

When the American people allow themselves to be "bamboozled" by British intelligence, or are merely fully unaware victims, themselves, of some British-orchestrated foreign or domestic policy hustle perpetrated against them and their nation, there is often a fatal price that innocent people pay—whether that be in Iraq, Afghanistan, Libya, Pakistan, or Parkland High School, Florida. Tens, perhaps hundreds of thousands of Americans today are dying from self-inflicted injuries, whether through suicide, death by opioids, or other means, apart from shootings, including mass shootings. More American lives are needlessly squandered in opioids-addiction-related deaths each year—59,000 in 2016 alone—than the United States lost in the entirety of the Vietnam War.

This is because the United States, through the ongoing illegal insurrection against the Trump Presidency, is being kept from giving its own citizens, in particular its youth, a productive future by working together with the nation of China, and with Vladimir Putin's Russia, in what is called "the Belt and Road Initiative."

A remedy is urgently required; it is also available. There must be a change in the American mind-set, a return to the characteristic "anti-colonial" mind-set of revolutionary thinking that Benjamin Franklin, Alexander Hamilton, Abraham Lincoln and Frederick Douglass, among others, represented. The true, abiding national purpose of the United States, to provide for the promotion of the General Welfare so that, through the improvement in the capacity of the sovereign individual citizen to participate in the advancement of the nation's physical and cognitive growth, his increasing freedom of thought and action becomes the indispensable natural resource by means of which the "more perfect American union" is achieved—this purpose must be again taught, that it again become known.

To do this requires a society devoted to the never-ending increase of the capacity of the individual, not to merely "have more," but rather to know more and to do more, in order to be more. To that end, *EIR* presents here the April 2001 article by Lyndon LaRouche, entitled "The Tragedy of U.S. Education: Shrunken Heads in America Today."

From the Mountaintop

In the very beginning of his article, LaRouche distinguishes between seeing the world from "inside-out" and "bottom-up," rather than seeing the world from the "top-down." LaRouche insists that the individual can, and must, locate the meaning of his or her individual life, and therefore the mind, from the standpoint of, not mere "in the flesh" present-tense self-interest, but as a great Classical writer or composer would, in one's "after the flesh" future self-interest.

This requires an "education of the emotions" to qualify that individual to engage in the passionate discovery and invention of new physical principles for changing mankind's self-government of the future. There is no "present time" as is commonly thought, which is why there are no "current events"; these are mere shadows, distractions intended to frighten the enslaved cave dwellers chained to their various electronic devices. There is only future history, including our future view of the past.

For the world-historical individual, such as an Albert Einstein, a Beethoven, or a Frederick Douglass, the idea of the future is a physical existent, not only in

New York Historical Society

Frederick Douglass

the mind of the thinker, but also in the non-cognitive domain of non-human nature, both living and nonliving. The American Constitution, which Frederick Douglass ruthlessly defended against all detractors, whether Confederate or abolitionist, in its Preamble's reference to ourselves and our posterity, established the perfecting of the future, "a more perfect union," as both the task and the birthright of all, regardless of lineage or ethnicity. Oligarchy, whether represented by a king, slave-master, banker, or anyone else, was despised and rejected. To be an American is to fight, continuously and relentlessly, until all citizens of one's nation know that they, also, must not only have the right, but also earn the responsibility, to be productively creative.

America is not merely a place. It is not a "geo-strategic territory." America is the process of continuous, never-ending perfection of the knowledge of the "physical principle" of self-government, as embodied in Gouverneur Morris' phrase "a more perfect union." All people, and only people, that are dedicated to that principle, are Americans. That is how Abraham Lincoln, Frederick Douglass, Ulysses Grant, and associated defenders of the Constitution, invented the modern United States through a second American Revolution, employing the then just-created Republican Party for that purpose. That is why Franklin Delano Roosevelt in 1932 posthumously recruited Abraham Lincoln to the Democratic Party, calling his policy, not a "New Reconstruction," but a "New Deal."

To this end, the example of Frederick Douglass demonstrates that there is no human being that cannot defy the most adversely compelling circumstances of even a constrained, imprisoned existence, to successfully shape the course of all world history, even perhaps in his lifetime, both in ways he or she can and cannot know. Slavery as a mental condition must needs yield to "freedom" as a mental condition—a transformation that Douglass discusses as having happened as soon as he had learned to read.

Douglass' role in speaking out for freedom for the

Irish people in a trip he made to that nation in 1845, at the age of 27; his break with the anti-Constitution Boston abolitionists, particularly William Lloyd Garrison, and later his break with John Brown on the eve of the Harpers Ferry raid; and his recruitment of over 180,000 African-American men (and some women) to fight for the Union, the Republic and the Constitution, were mere indicators of his greatness. He was the decisive factor, in personally demonstrating, by his very existence, not only the absurdity of the "congenital inferiority" of the African—a "sales pitch" that LaRouche thoroughly documents was invented by the Venetian Empire. Douglass also demonstrated the perfectibility of the Constitution of the United States, in his relationship with Abraham Lincoln.

Though they at times disagreed, their political intersection between the years 1856 and 1865—through the then-revolutionary project known as "the Republican Party," and then the Lincoln Presidency, which became the "Second American Revolution" in effect—was the embodiment of the "more perfect Union" of the Constitution's Preamble, written by anti-slavery advocate Gouverneur Morris of New York in 1789.

Blacked-Out History

It is unfortunate that the campaign to extirpate American history in general, including the extensive "original source writings" of that history's own major actors, from the United States educational curriculum over particularly the past 80 years, has also derailed the heroic but limited efforts by serious historians such as Benjamin Quarles, Carter G. Woodson, Joel Augustus Rogers, James Weldon Johnson, and the James Anderson cited by LaRouche in his article.

African-American History Month was never intended to be permanent by those who originally proposed it. Now, with the disappearance of Lincoln's birthday (February 12) and Washington's birthday (February 22) from the calendar, combined with the containment of the "Negro/Black/ African-American History Month" campaign of many decades, one wonders whether it might not be better, as a counter-assault to the British coup, to declare this present February "Blacked-Out History Month" and start a campaign to re-introduce all of the real, non-British filtered, revolutionary history of this nation to its youth and the broader population.

Because of the general erasure of that literary record from the minds of even the majority of America's history teachers, despite the best efforts, Freder-

ick Douglass is still thought of as an appendage to that Second American Revolution, rather than a central, if still unacknowledged, leader of it. As a result, Douglass has suffered nearly the fate of Cassius Marcellus Clay, a far more important anti-slavery figure in American History than John Brown or William Lloyd Garrison, and who has been "disappeared from the books" because of his role in the emancipation of both Russian serfs and American slaves, in a joint, international anti-British Empire project that American Ambassador Clay and Lincoln carried out with Russia's Czar Alexander II. Both Douglass and Clay were exceptional, successful American revolutionary fighters who acted on principle, named the right enemy, served the American Presidency rather than smaller interests, and won.

'Agitate! Agitate! Agitate!'

Douglass' fiery, often dangerous, denunciations of slavery were polemical presentations to primarily "white" audiences that often, when most successful, emptied the room. The following account appeared in the *New York Sun*'s edition of May 12, 1848:

"Frederick Douglass said that after an anxious and careful investigation into causes of the continuance of slavery in the land, he found that it was caused by too much religion. The people were too reverential Godward to be honest man-ward. There were hundreds of churches in all directions, full of men and women paying homage to God and exhibiting great piety. If any one of these churches were asked for a place of meeting, the answer would be that they were for God to use. The poor Southern slaves, with their backs streaming with blood and their hearts burning with the love of liberty, had no chance to arrest the sympathies of these sanctimonious parties. After giving the names of several Methodist Episcopalian clergyman who were slaveholders—women whippers—he inquired, was not his assertion correct? Why he continued, it is a notorious fact that men were sold to build churches—women were sold to pay the expenses of missionaries—and children were sold to buy Bibles. Episcopalians, the Presbyterians, Universalists, Unitarians, and the Methodists, are all in connection with and abettors of slavery. The American church is a brotherhood of thieves (great confusion, excitement, hissing and cheering).

"What is the man who seized the babe from the mother's breast and sells it into slavery, but a thief and a robber,—and did not these churches which tolerated such an act partake of the crime? Were they not thieves and robbers? (The speaker here had recourse to mimicry which he appeared to be a complete master of. He had some popular pulpit orator in his mind's eye; for nearly 1/2 the audience laughed outrageously, while the other half started on their feet to go away.) Whilst the ladies and gentlemen were moving towards the door in a very exciting mode, the lecturer addressed them thus— Suppose you yourselves were black, and that your sisters and brothers were in slavery, subject to the brutality and the lash of the atrocious tyrant who knew no Mercy—suppose, I

Soldiers from the 54th Massachusetts.

say, that you were free, and that your dearest and nearest relatives were in the condition that the Southern slaves are, and that the church sanctioned with infamy, would you not feel as I do? There is no use in being offended with me, I have a right to address you. There is no difference, except of color, between us. And as I said four years ago, I say now, I am your brother— (cheers and laughter)—yes I am, and although you may pass me by as you will, and cut me and despise me, I'll tell everyone that I meet, that I am your brother. (Cheers and laughter.)"

Douglass insisted on organizing everywhere he went, and in every waking minute he could devote to it, because his physical freedom could be taken from him at any time. Even in his 1845 voyage across the Atlantic, Douglass also took the opportunity to advocate, and to "agitate, agitate, agitate!" against slavery. In a letter to abolitionist (and anti-Constitution northern secessionist) William Lloyd Garrison, he wrote the following:

"Dear friend Garrison: thanks to a kind Providence, I am now safely in old Ireland, in the beautiful city of Dublin.... I know it will gladden your heart to hear that from the moment we first lost sight of the American shore, till we landed at Liverpool, our gallant steam-ship was the theater of an almost constant discussion of the subject of slavery—commencing cool, but growing hotter every moment as it advanced … It was a great time for anti-slavery, and a hard time for slavery; the one delighting in the sunshine of free discussion, and the other horror-stricken at its God-like approach."

By the time he had nearly reached Ireland, however, Douglass' debating partners were more than merely irate. They "actually got up a mob—a real American, republican, democratic, Christian mob … The clamour went on long after I ceased speaking. It was only silenced by the captain, who told the mobocrats if they did not cease their clamour, he would have them put in irons; and he actually sent for the irons, and doubtless would have made use of them, had not the rioters become orderly. Such is but a faint outline of an American mob on board of a British steam packet."

Douglass' emphasis on freeing oneself through the agency of reading and education, and on the vigorous, polemical, and often inconvenient exercise of that education on behalf of the cause of freedom, illustrates something said by LaRouche in "Shrunken Heads":

"Those who enjoy the right to a Classical humanist form of education, or its functional equivalent in self-education, are implicitly free; those who lack that education, are assuredly inviting, if not already suffering the conditions imposed upon virtual human cattle, even the conditions of slavery."

Douglass was born into slavery in Maryland, and through self-education made himself a writer, publicist and national conscience. His son, Lewis Henry Douglass, was born free in Massachusetts, joined the 54th Massachusetts Infantry Regiment in March of 1863, became a Sergeant Major, the highest rank then allowed for an African-American, saw combat and was wounded, and after the war became a teacher for the Freedmen's Bureau. Douglass's grandson, Joseph Douglass, born in 1871, was a renowned concert violinist who performed at the World Columbian Exposition in Chicago in 1893, also attended by his grandfather and poet Paul Laurence Dunbar. Joseph Douglass was also the first violinist of any ethnicity to record for the Victor Talking Machine Company, later called RCA Victor.

From the bull-whip seized from the slave-breaker, to the Union army-issued rifle, to the violin—that is a chart, of sorts, of the progress of perfecting the Union, between the years 1818 and 1893. These "machine tools" found in the hands of the Douglass generations between 1830 and 1880, show the efficiency of progress brought about, both in his own family, and in the whole United States, through the self-educated mind of Frederick Douglass.

Further, the election of hundreds of African-American former slaves, most of them veterans of the 1861-65 War to Restore the Union, to hold public office throughout the South from particularly 1868 through 1876, would only have been possible because of the personal response of America's Union veterans to the cause of freedom to which they had been recruited by Abraham Lincoln and Frederick Douglass's collaboration. In the aftermath of Lincoln's assassination and with the strong support of President Ulysses Grant, it was Douglass' quarter century of warrior advocacy of the Constitution and his educated agitation that preceded those Reconstruction-era elections that substantially shaped the subjective mind-set and set

Library of Congress

Frederick Douglass (1818-1895) is shown here with his grandson, concert violinist Joseph Douglass.

the internal standard for the best of those legislators, both African-American and otherwise.

The comprehension and use of the Constitution's Preamble, as though it were seen from the standpoint of what physicist Bernard Riemann called a "thought-mass"— *Geistesmasse*—was the subjectively creative machine-tool which Douglass wielded in a way that only Abraham Lincoln understood from the same "top-down" outlook. That, and only that, will be the basis upon which today's American citizens, who would not willingly be "fooled all the time,"—slavishly snookered by the constant British intelligence operations run against their Presidency—would educate themselves, with the assistance of *EIR*, to defend it.

The New Paradigm:
Lift Every Voice and Sing!

by Diane Sare

Make me thy lyre, even as the forest is:
What if my leaves are falling like its own!
The tumult of thy mighty harmonies
Will take from both a deep, autumnal tone,
Sweet though in sadness. Be thou, Spirit fierce,
My spirit! Be thou me, impetuous one!
Drive my dead thoughts over the universe
Like withered leaves to quicken a new birth!
And, by the incantation of this verse,
Scatter, as from an unextinguished hearth
Ashes and sparks, my words among mankind!
Be through my lips to unawakened Earth
The trumpet of a prophecy! O Wind,
If Winter comes, can Spring be far behind?
—Excerpt from Ode to the West Wind,
Percy Bysshe Shelley

On Eve of the New Paradigm: Chorus as Herald
Feb. 20—With the recent series of horrific mass shootings at schools across the United States, many American adults and children are gripped by the fear and horror that something is dreadfully wrong, but they don't know how to get at it. Governor Matt Bevin of Kentucky has correctly identified the role of violent video games, which glorify and reward the killing of people, as an important aspect of this phenomenon, but the problem and solution are deeper. As American statesman and economist Lyndon LaRouche has stressed repeatedly, in every area of policy making, as well as in science and art, the issue is, "What is the nature of man, and what distinguishes man from beast?"

Mankind is the only species on Earth that can willfully change its mode of existence to support a growing population at an ever increasing standard of living, as measured in terms of life expectancy, infant mortality, energy consumption, and happiness. That is, contrary to the British Malthusian tradition, thanks to human creativity, resources for human beings increase as long as there are new universal principles to be discovered and incorporated into technologies used by human societies. This will be the case until mankind has discovered everything there is to know about the nature of life and the universe! (Yes, that's right, there is *no end* to that process!)

Not only is mankind capable of transforming itself as a species to higher and higher levels of development,

EIRNS/Brian McAndrews   EIRNS/Brian McAndrews

LaRouche Youth Chorus, performing J.S. Bach's motet, Jesu Meine Freude at Lyndon LaRouche's Jan. 5, 2005 webcast from Washington, D.C.

EIRNS/Stuart Lewis

Diane Sare, conducting the Schiller Institute Chorus singing The Battle Cry of Freedom, at a Schiller Institute conference in New York City, Jan. 17, 2015.

but mankind must transform itself in this way, even to merely "survive." In fact, there is no such thing as mere survival. The only possibility is progress. To insist that mankind remain at any given level is evil, because it is counter to the nature of man. It is also impossible. A commitment to a so-called "sustainable" economy, means a commitment to a hyperbolic collapse, or even implosion of living standards and mass death. Thanks to the Congress of Cultural Freedom, that is where the United States is today. The death rate is actually increasing.

Happily, however, that is not the case for China and the dozens of nations now collaborating with China in President Xi Jinping's "One Belt One Road" initiative. President Trump, with his rejection of regime change wars, and his desire to do something to transform the standard of living inside the United States has opened the door to the possibility that the United States could join with China in President Xi's "Community for a Common

Destiny." The growth of Schiller Institute Choruses around the country, both in number and in quality, is indicative of not only the desire for such a "New Paradigm," but perhaps a glimmer of hope that it is also possible.

Lyndon LaRouche's Choral Project

When the LaRouche Youth Movement was at its peak recruitment phase in the first years after 9/11, LaRouche emphasized the necessity of choral singing, as part of an educational program. LaRouche emphasized the question of Italian *bel canto* technique, and placement of the voice, which is most naturally mastered at the Verdi mandated scientific tuning of C=256 Hz. He also insisted on the study of the principles of Classical composition, as opposed to popular "culture" or other arbitrary noise. J.S. Bach's *Jesu Meine Freude* became the laboratory for this endeavor, and the chorus became so unified, that when about a hundred members sang outside the Democratic Convention in Boston in 2004, delegates were certain that the chorus numbered in the thousands!

In October 2014, LaRouche announced his intent to

EIRNS/Sylvia Rosas

Schiller Institute Chorus performs Mozart's Requiem at the Co-Cathedral of St. Joseph on Sept. 11, 2016, in Brooklyn, N.Y.

restore Manhattan as the center of the United States (and his organization), as it had been in the time of Alexander Hamilton. By January 2015, a New York community chorus was being formed as an important part of this process. As the chorus grew and developed, it became clear that the process was having a deeply transformative effect on both the participants and the audiences, who were astounded to see their friends and neighbors coming together to produce a quality of beauty which they knew each person was incapable of producing alone, but whose participation was a necessary part of the whole.

The Sylvia Olden Lee Centennial Chorus. Concert on the hundredth anniversary of the birth of Sylvia Olden Lee, June 29, 2017, at Carnegie Hall in New York City.

In June 2015, in the weekly discussion with the LaRouche PAC Policy Committee, Lyndon LaRouche described the Thursday night "Fireside Chat" conference calls with hundreds of activists from around the country as a choral process, and compared that to the development of the Manhattan Chorus in the following way:

"Why don't we have a unified concept of chorus? Why don't we have a deep understanding, of the ancient Greek notion of chorus, because all great music comes, either from China or from Europe, in terms of the idea of the chorus. And the idea of the chorus is the unifying of a whole population to a common sense of reality and mission, whatever their other skills are. And they rejoice, they come together, and rejoice that they are coming together. And they go from whatever meetings they do and experience they have, and they feel refreshed by getting in that meeting, getting in that discussion, getting in that event, that musical performance."

A Nation-Wide Phenomenon

Schiller Institute Choruses are now growing across the country. The Manhattan process is the largest and has become an important voice in the affairs of the city and its people. The series of four performances of Mozart's *Requiem* in September 2016, as a "living memorial" on the 15th anniversary of 9/11, greatly elevated the dynamic of that moment, and resulted in substantial progress toward long overdue justice in that case.

On June 29, 2017 the Schiller Institute Choruses participated in a Carnegie Hall Tribute to Sylvia Olden Lee. It involved the Boston and Virginia Schiller Institute Choruses, as well as guests from Houston and Detroit, and an entire Harlem church chorus, making the combined chorus one of 220 voices. For everyone who participated, either as a singer or member of the audience, the experience lives on in memory, is unforgettable, and at concerts around the city, as soon as one brings it up, the other person says, "Oh yes, I was there," or "Yes, I heard about it, sorry I couldn't have attended."

The Manhattan Chorus also has participated in Choir Day celebrations in area churches, and a small group from the chorus now sings every Thanksgiving at a Rotary Club sponsored dinner for veterans in Harlem. After the terrible December 25, 2016 plane crash that killed 92 Russians, including the beloved Alexandrov Ensemble, members of the Schiller Institute NYC Chorus learned the Russian National Anthem and sang it outside the Russian Consulate, and at a special wreath laying ceremony at the Bayonne, New Jersey 9/11 Teardrop Memorial. They were joined by the Ceremonial Unit of the New York Police Department, the Bayonne Fire Department, and the Russian Deputy Permanent Representative to the UN, and this year, by the Syrian Deputy Permanent Representative as well.

These activities have not only had an important effect on the people of Manhattan and the people of Russia (the videos and news coverage of our memorials were widely circulated in Russia), but the chorus has become its own social dynamic, exactly in the way that

Schiller Institute

Schiller Institute Chorus members singing at the Russian Consulate in New York on Dec. 30, 2016, in memory of the beloved Alexandrov Ensemble after the Dec. 25, 2016 plane crash.

LaRouche described in 2015.

In October 2017, the Boston Chorus presented a concert of African American Spirituals and Classical Lieder at a church in Dorchester, commemorating the centennial of the births of Sylvia Olden Lee and John F. Kennedy, and the 250th birthday anniversary of John Quincy Adams. This church has now become an important collaborator in musical workshops, where the principles of Classical composition are being brought into the community. Members of the chorus have also been brought into classes at Berklee College of Music to present, through demonstration and performance, a conception of Classical culture in a school which mostly promotes jazz and rock music.

In Boston, as in Manhattan and Virginia, dedicated professional singers and teachers are joining our efforts to develop our choruses, and in Boston there is now an octet of our Boston musical leadership joined by some professionals, doing intense work on the Spirituals and the music of Bach.

In Virginia, the chorus is beginning to develop a much more unified character, helped by its collaboration with the Manhattan process and by its work on the Spirituals, whose apparent simplicity demands a profound unity of intent, since everything is transparent. The chorus has started a tradition of a New Year's Day *Musikabend*, which drew over a hundred people this year, including professional musicians, as well as local politicians and others.

In Houston, the chorus has been collaborating with community groups for Black History Month observations, as well as with diplomatic organizations, to promote the musical dialogue of the New Silk Road, in which our singers have been joined by musicians from China and other nations. At a recent Black History Month event, a pot luck of modern art songs, jazz, African drumming, and even rap, our chorus closed out the program with several *a cappella* African American Spirituals. This had a profound effect on the audience, many of whom approached our singers after the performance.

In Seattle the Schiller Chorus just gave a short performance outside the Korean Consulate, singing an arrangement of "Ari Rang," composed by a Schiller Institute member in Germany. The song is known as the "unofficial national anthem," and had been the national anthem before the division of the country. In preparing such a gesture of goodwill, the members of the chorus were inspired to strive for a superior performance, as they considered not only their own enjoyment of singing, but the powerful effect it could have on the Korean diplomats and other passers by to know that a group of Americans cared about the potential for peace to break out on the Korean Peninsula.

Renee Sigerson: It's the Nature of the Mind

Renee Sigerson, who grew up in New York City—and whose husband John Sigerson is the Artistic Direc-

EIRNS/Dwight Jarrett

A musical dialogue of cultures, Houston, Texas, May 16, 2017.

tor of the Schiller Institute NYC Chorus and Music Director for the Schiller Institute—had the following thoughts after the chorus participated in a Family Day celebration at the Harlem church of one of our chorus members. The bishop of that church, clearly a product of the type of education that Renee describes, was delighted to jump into the tenor section with his own, well worn copy of Handel's *Messiah* to join us in singing the Hallelujah Chorus. She reported:

"Since I grew up in New York City, and was deeply involved in the official music programs of the city from the age of 9 through 16 years old, I have a certain kind of reaction to what I've seen.

"Our work is really the leading edge for reversing the horrible attack on education that was unleashed in that critical U.S. city by the Ford Foundation in 1968, a few months after the murders of Martin Luther King and Robert Kennedy. On the one hand, the effect we are having awakens the potential for reversing the horrible setback induced by that manipulated Fall 1968 shock racial division of the city, artificially induced during the 1968 New York City Teachers' Strike. But the deeper implications are even more important. What we are tapping into raises the prospect of creating a more solid foundation behind education and culture, more broadly, so that the kind of nightmare which has settled over New York and other major U.S. cities can be finally ended in such a way that this never happens again.

"Music is critical for that prospect.

"Starting with the JFK Presidency, New York was one of the U.S. cities that built up a massive program of musical education. What was going on in the schools intersected the professional music world, the conservatories, and the universities. Music was everywhere—classical music. Every single junior high school in the city had an orchestra, many elementary schools had orchestras, and many of the music teachers were highly trained professionals who found the city's wage and benefits program far superior to the private orchestra contracts they had to compete for.

"In this environment, sustained by all kinds of ethnic communities, many of the absolutely best singers in the United States came from the churches and synagogues in that city.

"Most of this is gone today. The love of music is still there, but the programs have been hugely downgraded by the collapse of the education system. People are desperately trying to hold on to that essential life activity by programs that are at a much lower level of knowledge and ability than used to be common. Even when there is a more profound intention, music is being treated as an entertainment, a kind of 'Ed Sullivan' talent show event, where one hopes that someone with some training will finally deliver the gift.

"What we have begun to introduce is a phenomenon of reviving Classical musical culture around profound ideas and discoveries. This is generating a kind of ferment, a sort of bubbling excitement among people who want something better, but they don't want to let themselves and others down by demanding it. The way we are using the tuning as a foundation for a faster rate of progress in skills, and delivering the poetic content of the compositions we are gathered around, has awakened within all kinds of people a sense that something better and more far reaching is possible. The way we combine scientific discovery with poetry gets at the core of exactly what was missing in the past in the U.S. educational environment, namely a clear view of the difference between British Empiricism and the way it separates every area of knowledge into a little cubicle void of any universal content, and the Classical viewpoint that roots education in the matter of the nature of the human mind."

A Choral Destiny

This musical tradition in Manhattan can actually be traced back to the legacy of Alexander Hamilton and his conception of a unified republic. Manhattan was the natural location for Jeanette Thurber and her project for a National Conservatory of Music, which brought the talented singer Harry T. Burleigh into collaboration with composer Antonin Dvorak. Several of the musicians with whom we have been collaborating have very direct ties to that process, and to those particular individuals. However, but for Lyndon LaRouche's profound understanding of this principle, as expressed only in part above, that legacy might now be buried under this Dark Age culture which gave us the horror of the Parkland Florida killings.

Instead, as a result of LaRouche's decades of work to shape the presidency of the United States of America in the tradition of our Constitution—combined with the Chinese conception of a "community for a common destiny," already directly reaching Americans in such locations as West Virginia, Alaska, and Houston, among others—as the poet Percy Bysshe Shelley has expressed in many of his poems and essays, the Parkland tragedy may awaken a revolutionary Chorus among the people of the United States, who are just beginning to locate the placement of their long lost voice.

THE TRAGEDY OF U.S. EDUCATION

Shrunken Heads In America Today[1]

by Lyndon H. LaRouche, Jr.

It is a fair rule-of-thumb, that until he thinks of himself as just another victim of the situation which the legacy of Richard Nixon's "Southern Strategy," has re-imposed upon those fellow-Americans considered to be of African descent, no citizen of the U.S.A. is capable of seeing the reality, that his own rights as a human being are impaired by the systemic defects in our nation's present culture.

The truth of this matter, does not lie in the situation seen as the usual individual victim views it, as if with eyes in shrunken heads, from inside-out, and bottom up. Instead of the usually expressed, "TV talk-show" view of the issues, the individual must develop a scientifically efficient grasp of the centuries-long, even millennia-long historical process which has placed the victim, whoever you are, in that position.

We must view the situation of the victim, from outside himself, from the standpoint of considering his society as a whole, in which the individual exists only briefly as a mortal individual. What will be your continuing interest in the outcome of your mortal life, later? Thus, the meaning, and self-interest of that individual mortal life, could be competently conceptualized only as the principal authors of the 1776 Declaration of Independence and general welfare clause of the 1789 Preamble to the Federal Constitution situated the individual, only in two respects. Narrowly, by the individual's acting from the vantage-point of a top-down comprehension of that long-term historical process in which he is situated; but, broadly, by the individual's contribution to improving the culture within which his individual actions and their consequences are situated.

In the course of this report, I shall clarify that matter, of inside-out versus top-down, as a central matter of the scientific principle to be brought to bear; but, meanwhile, expect my proof, in a later part of this report, that the problem of racism in America today, could not be efficiently explored for durable solutions, without bringing in the issue of the top-down outlook.

As I shall show, the racism radiating from former President Nixon's 1966-68 launching of his "Southern Strategy," and permeating U.S. society, top down, today, is not a only a matter of society oppressing those considered as of African descent. It is an included symptom and product of the systemically oppressive, all-pervasive, degenerative, present condition of the society in which that specially oppressed stratum is nothing different than an integral part.

The problem immediately before us, is a matter of Nixon's abruptly reversing the trend toward civil rights, his reenergizing of a long-existing, axiomatic legacy of racist intention, as expressed in U.S. society at the moment of the assassination of Rev. Martin Luther King. This is an oppression which continues to be directed not only against so-called African-Americans, but against each and all of the members of our society, whether they are conscious of this state of their affairs, or not. The effects, already actual and worse threatened, produced by the presently accelerating, new general collapse of the world's present financial system and economies, are an expression of these connections.

As I shall show in this present report, the truth of the matter at issue is exposed, most efficiently, from the standpoint of studying those defective policies which are usually practiced in the often misused name of education, the policies experienced by nearly all students, in virtually all schools and universities, still today. It is in the footprints left by the trends of change in U.S. public and higher education, and the relationship of ed-

---

1. This was written for the included purpose of setting the stage for a coming, Bad Schwalbach, Germany conference of May 4-8, which will have as an included feature some deliberations on urgent contemporary issues of Africa itself.

The problem of racism in America today radiates from President Nixon's 1966-68 "Southern Strategy." It is not only a matter of the oppression of those of African descent, but expresses the pervasive degeneration of U.S. society. Right: Nixon with George Wallace in Alabama. Left: A policeman surveys the wreckage after the bombing of a black church in Birmingham, Alabama, 1963.

ucation to citizens' voting rights, rather than such matters as employment and housing as such, that the principled issues are most immediately and clearly expressed. Patterns of employment and housing can be changed; but it is only proper education, armed with their struggle to acquire and maintain voting rights, which can enable the victims of unfair practices in employment and housing, to change their situation in the only way possible, *politically.*

As a first step toward that knowledge, look over my shoulder, to see that problem, so defined, as my experience has shown it to be.

My first actual knowledge of the institution of racism in the U.S.A., came, more than seventy years ago, from the dinner-table discussions at the Ohio parsonage of my maternal grandfather, the late Reverend George Weir. For me, as a child, this repeated experience was like sitting, rapt, at the performance of a great Shakespeare drama; it was living history of a recent past century, brought to life, renacting itself before me. The dominant figure on stage in those dinner-table conversations, taken as a whole, was the family's vivid anecdotal memory of my great-great grandfather, the Rev. Daniel Wood, a Quaker abolitionist in the following of John Woolman, and a contemporary of Abraham Lincoln's generation, who had resettled in the area

north of Columbus, Ohio, in what is known as Woodbury. Rev. Wood had run one of the "underground railroad stations" in Ohio, and was known by handed-down family reputation as a "Henry Clay Whig" in his leanings. [2]

During my early years, first, in a Rochester, New Hampshire childhood, and, later, adolescence in the area of Boston, Massachusetts, my understanding of institutionalized racism in the U.S.A., was limited to what was supplied to me from a combination of certain Quaker traditions and my adopted, adolescent, self-identification as a follower of President Abraham Lincoln and his Clay-Carey tradition generally.

It was during my war-time experience, in military and related settings, that I had any first-hand encounter with the institutionalized contemporary practice of anti-"African-American" racism, in a more concrete,

---

2. George Weir was the teetotalling son of a professional Scottish dragoon, the latter equally adept with whisky and saber, who immigrated into the Fall River, Massachusetts area, circa 1861, to join the First Rhode Island cavalry. George Weir's uncle, Captain William Weir, was a Scottish sea-captain, who took the assignment of commanding a U.S.-made steam-ship from Rhode Island, down the Atlantic to Argentina. My paternal grandfather was a clever and energetic fellow of Quebec origin, but unfortunately a bit too soft on Clemenceau for my taste. A pedigree well suited to the requirements of an American Whig of the Clay-Carey-Lincoln tradition.

Henry Clay (1777-1852). LaRouche's maternal great-great grandfather, the Rev. Daniel Wood, ran an "underground railroad station" in Ohio, and was known as a "Henry Clay Whig" in his political leanings.

personalized way. My concerns on this matter were strengthened by experience with the disgusting racism exhibited by the British, military and others, in India and Burma, during and following World War II. However, it was memories of my conflict with the hegemonic variety of oligarchical culture of the Greater Boston area, already during my childhood and adolescence, which I mined, in my adult reflections, for the depth of background needed to understand the top-down, anglophile cultural influences, by aid of which racism and its associated effects are spread in the U.S.A. more generally.

The shortfall in most academic and other specialist attempts at comprehension of the issue of racism in America, is exhibited by most of what is written in the U.S. today on the subject of education and its required content in general, including the subject of the education of so-called "African-Americans." For example, I have on my desk a copy of James D. Anderson's *The*

Education of Blacks in the South, 1860-1935.[3]

The latter is, on balance, an amiable and valuable book, and a timely one for today's study, that chiefly because Anderson documents, anecdotally, and clearly, the statistical fact of a crucial difference, that expressed as *intention*, between education for freedom, as the figure of Frederick Douglass typifies the latter approach to U.S. chattel slavery historically,[4] and the contrary tendency of direction in education, notably that of Douglass' opponents. That of Douglass' opponents was intended to adapt most among its victims to acceptance of a more or less stereotyped future style of life, a life typified by the relatively lowest categories of employment, rather than the development of the individual as a citizen of a republic, in the fullest sense of the term.

However, the crucial problem, which, regrettably, prevented Anderson's effort from approaching the quality of "definitive," reflects his attempt to situate that important phenomenon within the wrong historical geometry, that of today's broadly accepted list of academic, so-called political-science categories, and, therefore, to ignore the essential, top-down features of the history of the relevant development of the policies and issues of education in the preceding approximately 2,600 years of European civilization. The overall result of those errors, is an example of the dangers of today's customary academic errors, of fallacy of composition in selection and treatment of the evidence considered.

I need not review Anderson's book itself here. I address the context in which I wish he had situated his approach to defining the deeper implications of the matter, and let the reader then read his book, this time in the context of the deeper issue which I set forth as follows.

1. Racism in Modern Society

Racism in the American colonies, and the U.S.A. itself, can not be competently understood, except as a product of the circumstances under which the imperial

---

3. James D. Anderson, *The Education of Blacks in the South, 1860-1935* (Chapel Hill: University of North Carolina Press, 1988).

4. The bell-wether of that book's shortfalls, is the lack of emphasis on the case of Frederick Douglass, which should have been a central feature of Anderson's treatment of the very subject on which he focusses.

A school at the Freedmen's Bureau in Richmond, Virginia, after the Civil War.

founder of empiricism, Venice's Paolo Sarpi,[7] the slave-trade became a typical practice among the customs of the Dutch and English India companies.

At the close of the Eighteenth Century, Britain began to dump the African slave-trade from vessels sailing under the "Union Jack," in favor of using the British merchant marine's bottoms for the East India Company's more lucrative opium traffic; but, Britain continued its participation in the slave-trade, deep into the Nineteenth Century, but then chiefly through its clients of the Portuguese and Spanish monarchies. In fact, the British monarchy has maintained the pro-genocidal legacy of that nation's slave-trade tradition, as Field Marshall Montgomery did, to the present day of British specialists Lynda Chalker's and Caroline Cox's currently continuing roles in shaping British and U.S. Africa policies.[8]

maritime power of Sixteenth and Seventeenth centuries Venice, the leading European opposition to the networks and legacy of Cardinal Nicholas of Cusa, organized the modern African slave-trade.[5]

That slave-trade began in earnest at the outset of the Sixteenth Century, following the death of Spain's follower of Alfonso Sabio, Isabella I, through Venice's political control over the Iberian maritime powers and their monarchies. This same Venetian influence, was also exerted during that period by such figures as Henry VIII's marriage counselor, Zorzi, who were associated, like the Plantagenet Cardinal Pole and the Newt Gingrich-like, Sir Thomas More-hater Thomas Cromwell, with the circles of the Paduan mortalist Pietro Pomponazzi.[6] Later, during the Seventeenth Century hey-day of the relevant

The characteristic feature of that modern slave-trade, is that it was premised on Venice's success in establishing a widely accepted convention as a "rule of law," *a presumed rule of international positive law, that any person of sub-Saharan African descent shall be defined as fair prey, to be made into a customary, and hereditary commodity and "shareholder value" of the modern slave-trade.* I refer to characteristics, distinct from the millennia-long, earlier practices of slavery, which first appeared in modern European civilization during the Sixteenth Century. This "rule of law" persists, in fact, as an active, and recently accelerated feature of the British monarchy's "Rhodes Plan" tradition of pro-genocidal policy of practice toward Zimbabwe

---

5. Nicholas of Cusa, 1401-1464, was a key figure of his century, who played a crucial role in establishing the modern sovereign nation-state and also in launching modern experimental physical science.

6. Francesco Zorzi (1466-1540); Henry VIII (1491-1547, reigned 1509-1547); Pietro Pomponazzi (1462-1525). The significance of the emphasis on "mortalist" here, is of crucial significance for grasping the origins of modern European racism. Although Pomponazzi's fear of the reprisals by religious authorities, and warnings to this effect by his student Gasparo Contarini, prompted him to appear to recant on this matter, his argument for mortalism is implicit in his elaboration of the Aristotelean method. In social practice, all of the leading Venetian currents were practicing mortalists. Slavery was one expression of this.

7. Paolo Sarpi (1552-1623).

8. Chalker and Cox have been key figures in the fomenting of genocidal conflict within sub-Saharan regions. Montgomery's Cecil Rhodes-echoing, homicidal statements on Africa policy are a matter of record, in his "Memorandum—Tour of Africa Nov/Dec 1947." See Linda de Hoyos, "African Unity: Community of Principle, or New Colonialism," *EIR*, July 30, 1999.

and other regions of sub-Saharan Africa today.

The doctrine of "Life, Liberty, and Property," of English empiricist John Locke, typifies the doctrine under which the institutions of slavery and "shareholder value" have been hegemonic among what President Franklin Roosevelt recognized as our nation's treasonous "American Tory" faction, the faction represented by the combined forces of the anglophile current centered within Wall Street, and those, such as the self-styled "Nashville Agrarians,"[9] filled with nostalgic yearning for the quaintness of the Confederacy.

The mere details of the historical record on the documentation of slavery and Jim Crow, are so extensively documented, that it would be superfluous to reprint that vast record as part of the present report. Useful as that documentation is for the purpose which it serves, such mere statistical and anecdotal documentation has so far failed, inevitably, to get to the crucial point of national policy at issue.

So much putatively scholarly and other attention, has been given to the interpretation of the emotionally charged phenomena of slavery and racism in America, that the most important side of the issue, *the causes for the interpreters' doubtful interpretation of that racism,* has been buried.[10] My point here, is to treat those interpretations of the facts as what they are, in net effect, often inflammatory distractions of attention from the underlying, determining, principled, functional features of the solution for the continuing injustice to be cured.

Therefore, I ask you to focus your attention on the axiomatic features underlying modern history as a whole. To this end, I focus upon that aspect of the practice of slavery, which has continued to be expressed as a continuing political alliance between the "American Tory" tradition of the southern slaveholders and New York-centered Anglo-American financier interest, down to its fresh upsurge as the Nixon-led "Southern Strategy," which has dominated U.S. policy-trends increasingly since 1966-1968.

I say again, for emphasis, that the tradition of slave-holder interest, as defined by John Locke and his followers, has a vigorous reincarnation as the Locke doctrine of "shareholder interest" today. On today's global scale, that Locke doctrine, deployed under the name of "shareholder interest," has become as murderous and savage a pro-racist killer, as the old Locke doctrine of "slaveholder value" took pride in being. I shall not, and need not repeat here what is documented sufficiently elsewhere, on the relevant subject of the legacies of Jeremy Bentham's Aaron Burr and Burr's Martin van Buren, as by Anton Chaitkin's ***Treason in America***.[11]

The Central Issue of Law

The precondition for any competent discussion of the practice and legacy of chattel slavery, and of the education of populations of former slaves and their descendants, must begin by locating the central principle of intention of law at issue in all these cases.

That issue of law is, that, prior to the revolutionary introduction of the principle of a modern sovereign form of nation-state, itself based on the principle of the general welfare, all known forms of society degraded most of their subjects to the status of either wild creatures to be hunted, or, as the Roman imperial Code of the Emperor Diocletian did, and as the feudalism of Venice and its Norman and Plantagenet allies did, that of virtual human cattle. Like cannibalism, head-hunting, and Phoenician infanticide, slavery was but one of the typical expressions of the bestiality of man to man, which pervaded known or inferrable history and prehistory, prior to the great moral improvement introduced during the Fifteenth-Century birth-pangs of modern European civilization.

For recorded portions of ancient, medieval, and modern Mediterranean and European history, the prototype of ancient societies, was the continuity of the model of ancient Mesopotamia (e.g., Babylon), the Delphi cult of the Pythian Apollo, and pagan Rome. These societies were sometimes identified as expressions of an "oligarchical model," and, whether described so or not, fit that standard description. It is the continued legacy of that oligarchical model, commonly expressed in modern times as *Romanticism,* which is the ancient systemic root of the evil of racism, and of related phenomena, in all of modern European civilization, including the U.S.A. today.

____

9. See Stanley Ezrol, "William Yandell Elliott: Confederate High Priest," *EIR*, Dec. 5, 1997; "Vanderbilt University and the Night Writers of the Ku Klux Klan," *New Federalist*, Oct. 7, 1996, p. 7; "Elliott and the Nashville Agrarians: The Warlocks of the Southern Strategy," *EIR*, Jan. 1, 2001.

10. Typical of such dubious interpretations, are the assumption that either sexual-cultural issues are determining, or that "white racism" is a reflection of so-called "Caucasians," and "black racism" a biologically determined cultural distinction of Africans.

____

11. Anton Chaitkin, *Treason in America: From Aaron Burr to Averell Harriman* (Washington: Executive Intelligence Review, 1999).

The introduction of the trans-Atlantic slave-trade into the Americas was aimed o prevent the successful development, in either the Americas or Europe, of the new form of independent nation-states modelled on the reforms of France's Louis XI and England's Henry VII.

The modern African slave-trade, as launched, under Venetian influence, near the beginning of the Sixteenth Century, was first practiced by Portugal and Spain, and later by the ruling oligarchies of the Netherlands and England, that according to the precedent of pagan Roman law (i.e., Romanticism). As noted, these modern slave-traders treated so-called "black Africans" as, originally, wild prey to be hunted, and the captives held, bred, and culled as, quite literally, human cattle.

Three features of this Venetian innovation in the practices of slavery, as by the Portuguese and Spanish monarchies, are most notable.

First, that the introduction of the trans-Atlantic slave-trade into the Americas by the Sixteenth-Century Portuguese and Spanish monarchies, and under the Seventeenth-Century Dutch and English monarchies, was aimed, from the beginning, to prevent the successful development, in either the Americas or Europe, of the new form of independent nation-states modelled on the reforms of France's Louis XI and England's Henry VII.

The included aim was to plant and develop in the Americas a powerful oligarchical class, of the *compradore* type, as typified by the English-speaking North American slaveholders and their confederates, which would both loot the Americas for the profit of their Eu-

ropean backers, and also serve to suppress the tendency toward emergence, in those Americas, of independent nation-state republics, the latter according to the Fifteenth-Century nation-state principle, the constitutional principle of the general welfare.[12]

The second feature, was the change in the way in which the virtually global marketing of African slaves and their produced product was practiced, relative to earlier periods in European history. The genocidal scale of loss of life among the victims, in their capture, culling, and transportation to the Americas, reflected the commercial programs used by Venice and its Portuguese, Spanish, Dutch, and English and French partners (chiefly). The appetite for the profit of such forms of looting, and the demands of those financier interests who funded these operations, resulted in a vast expansion of the scale of slavery; and the ratio of deaths caused, both directly and indirectly,

---

12. Although the first attempts to establish nation-states in Europe are typified by the efforts of Staufer emperor Frederick II, in peninsular Italy and Sicily, Alfonso Sabio in Spain, and the work and influence of Dante Alighieri, the first successes came directly out of work of Cardinal Nicholas of Cusa and his friends, in the context and aftermath of the great ecumenical Council of Florence. It was the Fall of Constantinople, in 1453, which impelled the circles of Cusa, such as his friends Fernão Martins and the astronomer Paolo Toscanelli, to launch what became known as the rediscovery and colonization of the continent and islands of the Americas. The included purpose of this project, and its included evangelization, was to outflank the combination of enemy forces, represented by Venice and the Ottoman Empire, by building up allies for modern European civilization in lands beyond the oceans. Thus, from the voyages of Columbus, the development of colonies in the Americas became a battleground between the pro-slavery Venetian faction, which took control of Spain's monarchy after the death of Isabella I, and the Christian forces of the Council of Florence. The battle between pro-slavery and anti-slavery forces in North America can not be understood competently as an historical phenomenon, except from this standpoint. The development of proto-republics in North America, beginning with the Massachusetts Bay Colony of the Winthrops and Mathers, and the continuation of that legacy under Benjamin Franklin and his circle, must be understood in light of that conflict.

Economist Henry Carey demonstrated that the pre-1861 U.S. economy did not profit from slavery, but, rather, lost money. It was the British monarchy that gained, by looting the U.S. physical economy, its people and its natural resources, for the enrichment of the parasitical British system. Here: a cotton plantation in Texas in the early 1900s.

by the combined capture and transport of slaves taken in Africa, zoomed to monstrous proportions.

The flooding of European markets with goods looted from the Americas and its growing slave populations, was, as has been generally recognized, a new, global, commercial scale and quality introduced to the practice of slavery.

This is a point addressed by the leading American economist, Henry C. Carey, in his work on the slave-trade and the practice of slavery in the United States. Essentially, Carey's facts show that the pre-1861 U.S. economy as a whole did not profit from slavery, but, rather, lost money on slavery. The net economic benefit of that slavery was enjoyed, not by the internal economy of the U.S.A., but by the British monarchy, looting the U.S. physical economy, its people, and its natural resources, for the enrichment of the parasitical British system.[13] The slave-owning U.S. planter class, was

simply a local pack of predatory parasites, compradores acting as the de facto agents of the British monarchy in this business arrangement.

The third feature, was the use of the power of the initially Habsburg-centered European assets of Venice, to attempt to crush the accomplishments of the Fifteenth-Century Renaissance out of existence in Europe itself.

Their intent was to destroy and outlaw that institution of the sovereign nation-state based on the principle of the general welfare, such as Louis XI's France and Henry VII's England, which had been introduced by the Fifteenth-Century European Renaissance. The roles of the Habsburgs, as tools of Venice, in both the fostering

---

13. Henry C. Carey, "The Slave Trade Foreign and Domestic," in W. Allen Salisbury, *The Civil War and the American System: America's Battle with Britain, 1860-1876* (Washington, D.C.: Executive Intelligence Review, 1992). Note, on the map of the Americas, the areas in which the practice of slavery was carried out in great concentration:

Brazil, the Caribbean islands, and the southeastern U.S.A. Then compare the vastly higher per-capita net product of agriculture in the northern U.S. states. Islands were ideal locations for controlling large slave populations; areas of relatively warmed climates and relatively dense rainfall were indispensable for operations in which wealth extracted meant chiefly a looting of land and human bodies alike. Hence, the irony of Nixon's "Southern Strategy," which, in thirty-five years, has transformed the formerly richest, most productive region of the U.S.A. into a "rust belt."

of the trans-Atlantic slave-trade and the religious warfare of the 1511-1648 interval, were continued through the participation of the Nineteenth-Century Habsburg and Spanish monarchies in support of the cause of the slaveholders in North America against the United States, through the point of that assassination of Lincoln, conducted with political support from Habsburg circles in Rome and elsewhere, through the 1863-1865 interval. The British monarchy, although a rival of the Habsburg-centered pro-feudalist interests of continental Europe, played the same role in its own interest, often in concert with its imperial rival, the Habsburg interest.[14]

Thus, the three pro-slavery factors so indicated, are fully congruent with the adopted legacy of the so-called "conservative revolution" of the modern fascist tradition traced from Romantics such as Friedrich Nietzsche and like-minded existentialists, through Mussolini, Hitler, and the neo-Confederacy tradition of Presidents Theodore Roosevelt, Woodrow Wilson, and the Nixon "Southern Strategy" campaign of 1966-1968.[15] As I have documented that point in an earlier published location, the Confederacy qualifies as a fascist state in the strictest sense, that of the 1789-1794 Jacobin Terror, the tyrannies of Napoleon Bonaparte and Napoleon III, and Twentieth-Century cases such as Benito Mussolini and Adolf Hitler, and their co-thinkers of the 1920-1945 interval. The "Southern Strategy"

is, as Newt Gingrich described his "Contract With America" movement, in 1995, a strictly fascist movement, a "conservative revolution," as Armin Mohler defined it as an historical phenomenon, in the footsteps of Robespierre, the imperial Bonapartes, Mussolini, and Hitler.[16]

That defines, summarily, the context, within which the history of the modern slave-trade and its aftermath must be situated, for any competent understanding of the roots of racism in America today. It is only against that historical background, that the issues of law and related policy may be competently addressed.

The fundamental issue of law posed by the legacy of that modern slave-trade, is nothing different than the following. *Is there some absolute difference, corresponding to a physical-scientific notion of a universal physical principle, between the nature of the individual human being and the nature of each and all lower forms of animal life?* It is from the standpoint of this question, and in no other way, that the issues of slavery and of education policy in general, are competently posed. As experience to date should have shown anyone alert to the facts, any different standpoint has turned out to be a dead end, and an awful waste of time, sweat, and much blood.

The fundamental issue, as I have just identified it, is best brought into focus by concentration on the way that issue is expressed in terms of policies for universal education.

The basis in law and custom for the institution of both the modern slave-trade and its continuing offshoots, is what I have already referenced here as that legacy of pagan Roman law and custom which is strictly definable as *Romanticism*. Empiricism, as associated with the legacy of Thomas Hobbes, John Locke, and Adam Smith, is the most widespread and important expression of Romanticism in the past and present history of the United States, and has provided the geographical basis, in choice of climate, for the legalization of the custom of slavery and the slave-trade within some among the original thirteen English colonies of North America, most notably the Carolinas, Georgia, and Virginia.[17]

---

14. This Habsburg anti-American tradition was defended by the Henry A. Kissinger (e.g., *The World Restored: Metternich, Castlereagh and the Problems of Peace 1812-1822* [Boston: Houghton-Mifflin, 1957]), who was trained at Harvard University under the neo-Confederate ideologue Professor William Yandell Elliott of *Nashville Agrarian* notoriety, as, implicitly, in his shameless London Chatham House address of May 10, 1982.

15. Theodore Roosevelt was raised as the nephew of the notorious Confederate spy and filibuster Captain James Bulloch. Woodrow Wilson was not only an unregenerate enthusiast for the original Ku Klux Klan, but played a leading role in reviving the Klan, publicly, from the White House, while President. President Grover Cleveland, a Democrat of the same political faction as Republican Theodore Roosevelt, orchestrated the changes in policy which led directly into the establishment of "Jim Crow." President Calvin Coolidge represented that faction in the Republican Party. Presidents Nixon and George Bush, Sr., have been an integral part of the "Southern Strategy" of racism, and the financier interests immediately associated with President George Bush, Jr., are fairly described as pro-racist, Southern-based carpetbaggers who have been looting the former agro-industrial power of the U.S. into a "rust belt" condition since Nixon's 1968 election. On the links to Nietzsche, et al., see Armin Mohler, *The Conservative Revolution in Germany (Die Konservative Revolution in Deutschland: 1918-1932)* (Darmstadt, 1972).

16. Lyndon H. LaRouche, "What Is Fascism, Really?," *Executive Intelligence Review*, April 13, 2001.

17. In the northern states of the union, the superior productivity of labor, per capita and per square kilometer, in agriculture and otherwise, was a reflection of a massive investment in development of the basic economic infrastructure of the locality and region. This included both

Since prior to Plato, the fundamental issue of law within globally extended European civilization, has continued to be the conflict between two axiomatically irreconcilable notions of law and government, between the Classical standpoint of natural law, as typified by Plato and the Christianity of the *New Testament*,[18] and that opposing, pagan tradition known today as the Romantic school of law, whose precedents included the customs of ancient Babylon and the Delphi cult of the Pythian Apollo.

It is only from that standpoint respecting law, that the phenomena of racism in modern society can be competently diagnosed.

The effect of the influence of various forms of Romanticism, in crippling the mental and emotional life of Americans, for example, generally today, is pervasive, and is expressed in varieties of ways. Empiricism, as typified by the teachings of Locke, as aggravated in the form of imported positivism and its offshoot, the pragmatism of William James and John Dewey, or the behaviorism of Watson, et al., is to be recognized as the corrupting, hegemonic current in present-day education, law, and scholarly practices, in the U.S. It is also, specifically, the prevalent basis in intellectual corruption for what has been taught as "political science" and "sociology," during the past century. My concern here is to show, how all of that is combined with a specific degree and form of force, in the phenomenon rightly distinguished as racism.

In the history of European civilization, this issue is best typified by the irreconcilable opposition, both in principle and in fact of practice, between, as I have said above, that Classical Greek tradition typified by the dialogues of Plato and by Christian humanism, on the one side, and what is called Romanticism, on the other. The key to understanding all of the leading features of approximately 2,500 years of European civilization to date, is the conflict between the Classical Greek tradition of Solon, Plato, et al., on the one side, and the oligarchical model of ancient Babylon and the Delphi cult of the Pythian Apollo, and also, the legacy of pagan Rome.

That conflict between Classicism and Romanticism, is key to any competent understanding of the roots and effects of the modern slave-trade and its legacy as racism in the U.S. today. This locates the point of reference from which to understand educational policies of practice as the *political* battlefield on which the most essential fight against racism must be conducted.

Those who enjoy the right to a Classical humanist form of education, or its functional equivalent in self-education, are implicitly free; those who lack that education, are assuredly inviting, if not already suffering the conditions imposed upon virtual human cattle, even the conditions of slavery.

Plato's Meno Dialogue

In addressing the issue of slavery and its legacy in the U.S. today, the typification of this difference, as expressed in education, is Plato's *Meno* dialogue, as the lives of Classicist Frederick Douglass and of his family typify that distinction with a special practical excellence. Whereas, as I shall emphasize here, those who tolerate such swinishness as the policy of not compelling students to expose themselves to the ideas of "dead, white European males" (DWHEMs) are, in fact, acting to defend and propagate the mentality of men and women who embrace the most essential features of slavery. The act of the fool who rejects study of the ideas of DWHEMs, must therefore reject the lesson of Plato's *Meno*, and thus defines himself as the fool whose part he is playing. The life of Frederick Douglass expresses the same connection emphasized by Plato.

The essence of the issue posed by racism, is to be located only in respect to that conflict between those two views on education. Either one takes the side of Frederick Douglass in that debate, or one is, in fact, dedicated to promoting what is recognized as the practice of racism, whether one believes that he, or she intends that result, or not.

The so-called African-American, for example, who

---

the infrastructure of production as such, and that, such as schools, essential for promoting the productive potential of the population. In the practice of chattel slavery, the source of the wealth taken by both the planter class and the foreign (British) interest which that class served as compradore, was the looting, by what is called "primitive accumulation," of natural conditions, both the land and the living bodies of the slaves. Thus, the slave-system kept moving on, from looted areas, into new areas for production by slaves. Only where the climate allowed such looting to proceed, at least for a time, was this feasible. Hence, the relative brutishness of intellect and morals typical of the regions of the U.S.A. in which the tradition of slavery lurks on, to the present day.

18. To simplify the point, I emphasize both the Gospel of John and the Epistles of Paul, and the role of those portions of the *New Testament* employed by J.S. Bach for his *St. John Passion* and *St. Matthew Passion*. These aspects of the *New Testament* typify Christianity's integration of the Platonic Classical Greek cultural tradition into Christianity; Bach's referenced works, strictly reproduced in performance, express, most powerfully, the role of what Friedrich Schiller defines as *the sublime* in Christianity's notions of the Crucifixion.

defends the notion of an education free of the requirement of mastering the ideas of "dead white European males," is being a racist to himself; he is the slave who does not need to be enslaved, because he zealously puts his shackles on himself, and displays them proudly, even militantly. He is like that slave who insists, "Don't give me freedom; just give me reparations—money."

As Plato illustrates the proof of this, in his *Meno*, all human individuals have the developable cognitive potential to generate validated discoveries of universal physical principle. From that vantage-point, all human beings are equal in respect to their inborn nature, and all groups of human beings, from every society, share, as a group, that developable potential in virtually equal degree. The essential function of education, and of the conditions of family and community life in which education occurs, is to develop precisely that cognitive potential to the highest possible degree, in every possible young individual.

No lower form of life has this potential; that is the essential difference between man and beast. Beasts can learn, but only human beings can know; education which teaches children to learn to pass tests, to acquire habits needed for a specific form of employment, is education designed for beasts. Such forms of education, or of family relations, will tend to bestialize the students, and produce corresponding rations of bestialized adults. Unless your children are enjoying a Classical humanist form of education, they are being cheated; they are being bestialized, at least relatively so, that in the name of education.

It is important to emphasize, once more, that the result of accepting mere learning as a substitute for knowing, is not far from the condition of being a slave. At the very best, mere learning is a kind of obedience-training, as at a school for dogs, which produces an individual prone to many of the characteristics of behavior of a slave, the characteristics of a class of virtual human cattle.

Those who enjoy a Classical quality of education, and who are permitted to express that development in their practice as functioning members of society, are relatively "free," at least within and among themselves; those who lack such educational development, are not yet free within themselves.[19] Those who are not free within themselves, will find themselves, if not actually slaves, self-degraded to a condition fairly described as "human cattle," as today's U.S. popular opinion and mass entertainment, condition most Americans today to behave as did the Roman mob of spectators in the Colosseum, as human cattle, most of the time.

Now, turn again to Plato's *Meno* dialogue. Do not merely read it; relive it. Relive it as if you were, alternately, playing the part of the boy, and of Socrates: not acting out the recitation of the words, but reliving that experience of the paradox and discovery for which those words are, like sense-perceptions, mere shadows cast on the irregular wall of a dimly lit cave.

2. Education & Humanity

All of my own original discoveries of principle, during the approximately sixty years of my adult life, have been the harvest from a single germ, a germ whose existence I can date consciously, as a matter of knowledge, to no later than my childhood's family and community life, during my first three years of public school, in Rochester, New Hampshire. Some of the resulting, original discoveries, which first occurred early during my adult years, are shown to have been of outstanding, world-wide importance today, most emphatically so by the implications of the eruption of the presently ongoing, global, combined, existential financial, monetary, and economic crisis.[20]

---

19. Public and higher education in the U.S.A. provided the more fortunate pupil a map of some of the crucial topics which should be known. Unfortunately, that map concentrated on the student's learning to recite the map, more often than actually knowing the discoveries to which the points on the map corresponded. If the pupil's entire education provided encounter with a few teachers who provoked the pupil into the kind of experience of knowing typified by the *Meno* dialogue, the student was thus prompted to apply that lesson to the effect of developing his, or her own self-education. Read the map, but discover the actual territory to which the map pretends to correspond! Then, go on to build a corrected map. The difference is typified, as I stress in my "Gravity of Economic Intentions" (*EIR*, March 30, 2001), by the difference between the student who has *merely learned* to recite the Newtonian version of gravitation, and he who has relived Kepler's step by step process of actually making the original discovery of universal gravitation. Knowing, like food, nourishes the body; that which is not food, such as mere learning, will, in its best performance, merely pass the course.

20. Among increasing numbers of leading circles around much of the world, the relative uniqueness of my successes as an economic forecaster, and in related matters, is no longer honestly debated among competent observers. Since that fact, and its implications are fairly established, it is not necessary to plead a case which has been, thus, already proven. There is a point, beyond which, the assertion of denial becomes either factitious lying, or conduct beyond the bounds of reasonable ignorance.

As I have repeated that observation many times, it was during those childhood years in Rochester, that I recall today, reaching the conclusion that my parents, and most of the adults and peers I knew, lied habitually most of the time, as most of your friends and neighbors, and elected officials, still today.[21] It was also clear to me, that teachers, even then, were not necessarily a source of truthfulness. In my parental household, lying was filed, euphemistically, under such categories as "company manners," or falsehoods which, when caught out, were explained to the children as "I am only telling you this, for your own good." In school, the same type of practice prevailed, and tended, in my experience, to grow worse, not better, as the grade-levels succeeded one another.

In political life generally, lying is often called today, "Going along to get along." Dale Carnegie's ***How To Win Friends and Influence People***, is an example of a ritual devotion to lying, as seen through the eyes of my own generation.[22] "Sensitivity," is the code-word for widespread practices of lying popular among the so-called "Baby Boomer" generation. Those horrid, existentialist fanatics, who insist upon threatening school pupils with the Orwellian dogma, that there is no truth, only opinion, are perhaps the worst of the liars to be considered for the purposes of this report.

I recognized that what I was instructed to learn, was morally worthless to me, even if it might happen to be true factually, *unless I knew it to be true by my own intellectual resources*. I became, therefore, with but extremely rare exceptions, typically, the most knowledgeable person in any class I attended, among those most stubbornly resistant to merely learning what was prescribed. Some learned much more than I knew, but what I knew, I, unlike those peers, actually knew. I developed, more and more, the habit, that to say what one had merely learned to say, as to assert, as a matter of claims to *knowledge*, "What I read," or, "What I have been taught to believe," or "What I have been told by authorities I respect," is, itself, intrinsically, a form of lying, a form of habitual lying typical of the society and peer groups I knew.

Take, as an example, my rejection of the first year of

high school geometry, from about the first day of class.

Earlier, I had observed carefully the structures seen during one among my not-infrequent family visits to the Charlestown (Boston), Massachusetts Navy Yard, and recognized that the holes made in the steel beams made the structures stronger, by eliminating the burden of weight not essential to the function of supporting the structure itself. Why should people concerned with the strength of the structures they had constructed, make those holes in the relevant beams? I decided that knowing the kind of geometry required for this use of materials, represented some principle to be discovered and mastered.

So, when the teacher challenged the members of the assembled geometry class to identify the useful purpose for studying geometry, I referred to the effect of making those holes in the beams seen at the Navy Yard: one cuts out the holes to make the structure stronger; there must be some reason why circular, or approximately circular holes had been chosen for those cases. Those who ridiculed my response, which included some teachers at that high school, and most of the classmates, were not only clearly wrong on this and other issues expressing the same matter of method. This intellectual, and moral flaw expressed by my critics in that matter, is but all too typical of much of the adult population, even university science graduates with what are called, sometimes ironically, "terminal degrees," of the present day, and pathetically so.

In all my own teaching of university students, and in my leading role in the philosophical association which I have led, since more than three decades ago, I have recognized, and emphasized the importance of the individual's developing an epistemologically competent, critical insight into the characteristic panoply of ideology of his or her own culture, and of comparing the pathological quality inhering in that and all other ideologies of all cultures. Without that kind of self-conscious awareness of the invariably, ideologically polluted character of the prevalent assortment of leading ideologies within one's own cultural background, one is like a blinded beast struggling to survive in a swamp whose quicksands and other perils one is conditioned not to recognize.

Look at my immediate, and continuing disgust, in reaction to that classroom situation, from the standpoint of my frequent use, over recent decades of teaching and related activities, of the example of Johannes Kepler's original discovery of the principle of universal gravita-

---

21. The most important forms of lying in the three constitutional branches of the U.S. Federal government today, are lies made on the same pretext invoked by the spectactors of the pagan Roman Colosseum: "Go along, to get along."

22. Dale Carnegie, ***How To Win Friends and Influence People*** (New York: Simon and Schuster, 1936).

tion. The issue, that geometry must be studied from the standpoint of physics, rather than Euclidean ivory-tower geometry, was the same, in my relatively primitive, but accurate, adolescent's recognition of a pervasive, axiomatic fallacy in the classroom teaching of geometry and mathematics, and in Kepler's much more profound grasp of the same distinction, he echoing thus the insights of such among his named, relatively immediate predecessors as Nicholas of Cusa and Leonardo da Vinci.

Riemann's fundamental contribution to all modern physical science, was to free geometry from all such ivory-tower assumptions, and to base mathematics exclusively upon experimentally validated discoveries of universal physical principles. In my own principal original discoveries, I established the basis which enabled me, shortly thereafter, to view Riemann's work in the more general way required for a competent science of physical economy. It is mankind's relationship to the universe, as measured by increases in society's increased power to exist, per capita and per square kilometer of surface area of Earth, which is the foundation for all that truly sane people will regard as empirical knowledge, nominally physical-scientific or other.

That is the continuing tradition of Plato, Cusa, Kepler, Leibniz, et al., within which lie all of my principled contributions to society. So, the germ of all that began for me, in my rebellion against the kind of knee-jerk-reflex lying I witnessed, as a child, among my parents' household and their society. Herein lies also the germ of what must become our nation's general policy, respecting education for freedom.

As Kepler emphasized this fact, the astronomers Claudius Ptolemy, Copernicus, and Tycho Brahe, had each made the same specific mistake against which I rebelled in the secondary geometry class, as I rebelled, later in my student years, against swallowing a version of a differential calculus premised fatally upon the fraudulent, radically reductionist Cauchy "fraction," and as I, still later, in early 1948, rejected the fraud of Norbert Wiener's "information theory:" in each case, on the same epistemological premises.

There is no exaggeration, or other incongruity, in my comparison of my adolescent reaction against the underlying error of secondary geometry instruction, to the reaction of Kepler to the fundamental errors of method by Ptolemy, Copernicus, and Brahe. *What I expressed in that act of rebellion, was like Kepler's recognizing the fallacies of Ptolemy et al., a defense of that*

same principle which is innate to all human beings, and which expresses the fundamental distinction between man and the apes. This, as I shall emphasize, is, as Frederick Douglass's life reflects this, a distinction inhering in every child of those liberated from slavery, or of newborn children of today. This was expressed for me, as an adolescent, and also earlier, by a feeling of moral wrongness in the demand that one suppress in oneself the impulse to know, a demand that I do so for sake of the rewards proffered for obedience to the demand that one submit to learn as one is told.

More and more, especially as they grew older, most among those who had been my youthful peers capitulated, sooner or later, to the pressures for doing as one is told one must learn to do, especially as they acquired more and more of the burden of what are sometimes described as household life's hostages to fortune. The difference was, essentially, that I, like others of my kind, did not capitulate; being human was too important for us, to betray our birthright.

I shall return to that point as the pivotal feature of the argument developed in this report.

These three, Ptolemy, Copernicus, and Brahe, had constructed their astronomy on the basis of completely arbitrary, wrong-headed blind faith in the assumption, that events in space and time were organized according to a so-called Euclidean, infinitely linear, unscientific,[23] ivory-tower notion of space and time. Kepler, showing that any such construction as theirs, could not account for the variations in position and speed of the planet in its orbit, discovered an underlying, universal physical principle, universal gravitation, a discovery through which we are able, today, to *know* much about why the orbit behaves as it does.[24]

By "know," I mean, first of all, discovering paradoxical evidence, the kind of evidence which shows that reality contradicts absolutely what ivory-tower assumptions, such as those of Ptolemy, Copernicus, and Brahe, assume, still today, to be universally true. I mean also, solving the paradox posed by that contradiction; I

---

23. My use of "unscientific," here and elsewhere in this report, signifies arguments based upon included arbitrary assumptions, including those of Euclidean geometry, rather than methods appropriate for defining universal physical principles.

24. LaRouche, op. cit. The thread of development of this principle of method, as applied to this problem by Kepler, is traced explicitly from Plato, through his follower Eratosthenes, and from Nicholas of Cusa, through Leonardo da Vinci, Kepler, Gottfried Leibniz, Abraham Kästner, Carl Gauss, and Bernhard Riemann.

Join with LaRouche 65

mean, discovering, or rediscovering, through the perfectly sovereign cognitive powers of one's own individual mind, a Socratic form of *hypothesis*, which can be shown, physically, to be universally true, and is, therefore, an experimentally validated, universal physical principle. What you know in that way, and only in that way, is as much as you actually *know* about anything.[25]

This quality of *knowing*, as distinct from the beast-like ability *to learn*, is, once again, the essential, absolute distinction which sets the human species apart from all lower forms of life. In theological terms, this is the specific quality of the human individual, which is reflected in **Genesis** 1: man and woman as made equally in the image of the Creator of the universe, and, thus commanded to assume dominion within that universe, that in accord with the human individual's kinship to the nature of the Creator. This is no mere hand-me-down tradition; it is a scientific fact, as readily demonstrated as if that chapter of **Genesis** had never been written; sometimes, as the Apostle Luke writes, we must "let the stones cry out!"

Unless our natural human potential has been crippled by habituation to mere learning, when we, as such human beings, are faced with a paradox, in which something we had been taught to accept as universally true, such as a Euclidean geometry, is demonstrably false to physical reality, we reject the presumed authority of that mere learning. If we are then honest with ourselves, we cease to look for answers in "the back of the textbook," and cease attempting to pass the course by reciting what we have been taught to say.

Unless we are crippled by conditioning to accept conditioned learning, if we have not, like the Biblical Esau, sold our birthright for the mess of pottage called learning, we cease playing the game according to what we were told were "the accepted rules." We must strike out on our own, and discover a truthful solution.

However, this is no license for existentialism, or of kindred, inherently destructive, and evil forms of intellectual anarchy. In such matters, we must always act on behalf of discoverable truth, according to principles lacking in all beasts. We must act according to that specifically anti-reductionist quality of mind, which is in-

dicated by a literate use of the term *reason*, reason, sometimes called *natural law*, as pointing toward some imperfectly known, but coherent set of principles underlying the ordering of the universe.

How shall we know that the crucial solution for a rigorously defined paradox, called a Socratic hypothesis, which we believe we have uncovered, is truthful? Plato's **Meno** dialogue confronts the reader with precisely such a problem, and that in the form a slave boy might be capable of not only solving the problem, but know that he had solved it. There, in that example from Plato's work, lies the open door to a real education, a Classical mode of primary, secondary, and higher education.

I had the good fortune to meet a few teachers, in the course of my childhood and adolescence, who sometimes walked me through vivid experiences of discovery of the relatively simplest quality of universal physical principles, those of the type which the **Meno** and **Theaetetus** dialogues typify. In later life, Professor Robert Moon was notable among those whose impact upon me was of that quality.[26] With a bit of such help, here and there, what did most of the rest for me, were a similar approach to study of books and my own critical, experimental view of what became an increasingly rich experience of, and appetite for the world at large.

Once one has that kind of Socratic experience, as a child, perhaps one never really forgets it. In the first moments one is aware that one has confronted an actual paradox, produced the fruitful hypothesis, and proven the hypothesis by appropriate experimental standards, one must never forget that mental-emotional experience. It is something of a different quality than one experiences in any other way. That way of looking at the world, in terms of that special kind of cognitive experience, must become the core of our sense of "Who I am!"

In search of that truth of reason, about the age of twelve, I found myself lured into stumbling, as if purblind, but not accidentally, into a habit of reading phi-

<hr>

25. ibid. On *Analysis Situs*. This issue of method, was the thematic subject of the founding work of modern experimental physical science, Nicholas of Cusa's **De Docta Ignorantia**. It is the method of Plato, as richly developed, after Cusa, by Luca Pacioli, Leonardo da Vinci, William Gilbert, Kepler, Leibniz, Kästner, Gauss, Riemann, et al.

26. Robert James Moon (1911-1989) expressed his intention early in life to master thermonuclear fusion. Arriving at the University of Chicago in 1928, he was directed to William Draper Harkins at the Department of Physical Chemistry, with whom he studied and worked, later also obtaining an advanced degree in physics. He taught both subjects at the university. Professor Moon built the first cyclotron at the University of Chicago; solved the problem of the contamination of the carbon moderator, which made the Chicago pile possible under the wartime Manhattan Project; and, conducted pioneering research on the action potential of the nerve after the war, using the world's first scanning X-ray microscope, which he had designed and built.

losophy, and, increasingly, debating, within my mind, with the authors of those writings.

During the ages of twelve through eighteen, I worked my way through the standard books authored by each of those certified to me as the leading English and French philosophers of the Seventeenth and Eighteenth centuries. At the same time, I became more and more engaged by the writings of Gottfried Leibniz, and faced the challenge of Immanuel Kant's attack on Leibniz. About my fourteenth year, I had become a convert to Leibniz's approach, with special attention to the ***Theodicée*** and ***Monadology***, and by sixteen had begun filling notebooks with composed arguments in defense of Leibniz against Immanuel Kant of the Kemp-Smith presentation of the first and second editions of Kant's ***Critique of Pure Reason***.

The issue was the same which arose, during that same adolescence, as my quarrel with the ivory-tower version of Euclidean geometry, at the beginning of the high school geometry course. What are ideas, and what is the provable relationship between ideas and the physical reality of the universe upon which we are acting willfully?

In fact, I knew virtually nothing, first hand, of Plato's work at that time, or for some time later, but I had become, through my objections to the empiricists (among whom I included Kant), an implicit Platonist, through the mediation of English translations of Leibniz, and through wrestling, as if in living controversy on the stage of my imagination, against the principal philosophers of the so-called English and French Enlightenment.

The point to emphasize is that with which I began the present section of this report: How does one find one's way, in a world in which parents, teachers, peers, and public officials, lie about almost anything, most of the time? For an "ugly duckling" like me, that was the most important, the most impassioned, of all questions. It is the crucial issue, for any student, of securing an education for the cause of freedom.

It is necessary that I continue a bit longer here in this direction, but I shall interrupt the part of the development of my argument for a moment, now, to make some needed remarks on the direction in which this report is now leading us.

Classical Education

What I have just illustrated by these autobiographical references, illustrates, both technically and morally, what is meant by *a Classical humanist mode of education*, as Classical humanist education differs from those sundry Romantic varieties and their offshoots, which predominate in the schools, universities, and popular culture of the Americas and Europe today. I emphasize Classical humanist education, against the satanic influences exerted in U.S. and other educational policy today, by truth-hating existentialists such as the Nazi philosopher Martin Heidegger and his morally degenerate cronies Theodor Adorno and Hannah Arendt.[27]

The illustration I have given from my personal experience, just above, is typical of the importance of choosing the Classical humanist approach to classroom education, and also, toward the conduct of that greater portion of any successful Classical education, which must, of necessity, occur in the private, personal activity of the student, apart from the classroom.

The Classical education program, as conducted in the classroom itself, could provide no more than a good partial map of extant knowledge; the broader significance of the in-classroom program, is that it provokes the student to explore, on his own, the larger physical reality which the map attempts to represent, a map which is merely an approximation. A good Classical education, if constantly reenforced by an active, cognitive form of experimentally oriented self-education of that quality, develops in one the ability to make clear distinctions, as I did in my reaction against ivory-tower geometry, between a mere map and the physical reality which it, at its best, merely symbolizes.

The dialogues of Plato, the scientific writings of Archimedes and of his contemporary Eratosthenes, and the founding of modern experimental physical science by Cardinal Nicholas of Cusa, with his ***De Docta Ignorantia*** and relevant later writings in this field, the notebooks of Leonardo da Vinci, and the writings of Johannes Kepler, especially his ***New Astronomy***, are, if combined as one experience, paradigmatic for any serious student today. All great scientists, and all truly promising students, as children and adolescents, are those training themselves, primarily, in the role of becoming ever better performers as original thinkers, discoverers of experimentally validatable universal physi-

---

27. Theodor Adorno, et al., *The Authoritarian Personality* (New York: Harper, 1950).

cal principles, first, and pedagogues only as a subsumed part of the work of ongoing attack upon, and sharing of ever new discoveries.

As I walked readers through the successive steps of the process of such discovery, in sundry earlier publications, there are *three crucial implications of making, or communicating a series of validatable original discoveries of universal physical principles.*

First, what is the process by which a discovery of an experimentally validatable universal physical principle is made, and communicated, as such communication should occur between teacher and pupil in a competent form of education? I summarize here, what I have presented many times in earlier locations on the definition of *ideas.*

Second, what is different about such discoveries of principle, on the one side, and the objects we believe that we have experienced directly through the means of our sense-perceptions, on the other?

Third, when we take into account the ability to generate and communicate the experience of valid discoveries of universal physical principle among the members of society, what is the fundamental difference, on principle, between relations among animals, and among human beings? What happens to the notion of "race," once that difference is taken into account?

It is upon those three considerations that the notion of a Classical humanist mode of primary, secondary, and higher education is premised. It is in such a mode of education, that the otherwise infectious bestiality of notions of "race" is avoided.

Lately, we have been presented with paleontological relics, which anthropologist Meave Leakey claims to represent human life in Africa from several millions of years ago. I would not insist that she is mistaken in saying that those relics are representative of the human species, but the ideology of the school of anthropology with which she is associated, does not permit us to trust her on the matter of defining the nature of the strict difference between human beings and what are classed as "the higher apes."

Her argument, as I witnessed it on a televised interview broadcast by Britain's *Sky News,* is highly provocative, because of some among its more plausible features; but, the argument I heard from her is not definitive.[28] Perhaps there are physiological characteris-

tics of man as a cognitive species, which should indicate to us, as Leakey claims, even in the case of fossils, whether or not the fossil is human. We know that that kind of distinction has not yet been determined scientifically, *since the crucial question defining the relevant experiment has not yet been recognized among the relevant peer-review establishments.* Meanwhile, what we can classify as human fossils, are cases in which the site in question is conclusively associated with products of distinctively cognitive activity, of which, despite Wolfgang Köhler's use of the term "insight," higher apes are not capable.[29]

As a wag might put the point: "Teacher! Don't you monkey around with my children!"

This distinction goes to the heart of my original discoveries in the science of physical economy. What I personally, have to add to the extensive literature on the otherwise known principles of Classical humanism, is the effect of my discoveries in enabling us, today, to resolve certain previously unresolved issues of that topic. It is those resolutions which have made possible the fresh argument on education for freedom which I present here.

Now, focus on the three points I have listed a short space above. I turn now to the first of those topics, the subject of the act of discovering and communicating a valid discovery of universal physical principle.

Discovery & Its Communication

As I have elaborated this definition in locations published earlier, there are three distinct steps in any valid discovery of a universal physical principle. As I have summarized the point in those locations, the most appropriate presentation of that process of discovery references the practical significance of what Leibniz

---

pus platyops, which they say lived 3.5 millions years ago. Their claim is based on analysis of a skull found in 1999 in Kenya. What is clearly plausible, is the existence of humans in that part of Africa as early as three to four millions years ago, or even earlier, since the biogeochemical preconditions for human life have pre-existed for not less than approximately two millions years of recurring cycles of glaciation on much of the land-mass of the northern hemisphere. Obviously, the Indian Ocean region and its African coastal region are likely places to find human traces during, for example, the period of massive glaciation of the Eurasian and North American land-mass. However, it is one thing to know that human cultures' existence that early, or earlier, is plausible, and another to assume that a fossil is human, rather than a relic of some higher ape.

28. Meave Leakey and her daughter Louise announced on March 21, that they had discovered a new species of hominid, dubbed *Kenyanthro-*

29. Wolfgang Köhler, **Gestalt Psychology** (New York: Liveright, 1992, reprint of 1947 edition).

termed *Analysis Situs*, a notion which Riemann addressed explicitly, or otherwise, in all of his leading work. The most rigorous form of recognition of the need to effect a new discovery of universal physical principle, is the following.

Given an assumed set of definitions, axioms, and postulates, which have been assumed to best represent, mathematically, the consistent understructure of our prior knowledge of the physical universe. In the case, that an experimental, or equivalent experience, described strictly in those mathematical terms, produces a certain type of clash of represented results, we must regard that conflict as of the form of what we call an *ontological paradox*. Take as an example of this, Fermat's introduction of the notion of a contradiction between the notion that action occurs along a pathway of shortest distance, and the physical evidence, that refraction of light occurs along a different pathway, that of quickest time.

This discovery, as pursued further by Huyghens, Leibniz, Bernouilli, et al., required the overturn of that Aristotelean-Euclidean notion of mathematical physics which subsumes the neo-Ockhamite variety developed as English empiricism by Paolo Sarpi, Sarpi's houseservant Galileo, et al. That discovery did not provide the accomplishment of that task; it posed the need to develop a solution for that paradox. The combined effects of Kepler's and Fermat's discoveries, thus foredoomed the conventional classroom doctrine of geometry used in the usual mathematics and physics classrooms. The search for a solution for these paradoxes, led, as through the definitions of an anti-Euclidean geometry by Leibniz follower Abraham Kästner, through the work of Monge, Gauss, et al., to the discovery and development of modern hypergeometry, successively, by Gauss and Riemann.

To restate and emphasize that point in broader terms of reference: As I have indicated, in earlier locations, during the middle of the Seventeenth Century, this paradoxical experimental discovery by Fermat, juxtaposed against the paradoxes posed by the revolutionary discoveries by Kepler, set into motion all of the subsequent principal progress in physical science and mathematics, through the circles of Christiaan Huyghens and Leibniz, through the work of Riemann and beyond. Leibniz's originality in discovering the calculus, and his continuation of that discovery as his monadology, contrary to the later frauds by Leonhard Euler, Augustin Cauchy, et al., is a central feature of that process of de-

velopment. This would be a pivotal feature of any competent secondary-school program of education in mathematics and physics.

In any truthful, Classical secondary educational program, the student should relive Kepler's, Fermat's, Huyghens', Leibniz's, and Bernouilli's related work, as a mandatory exercise, prerequisite to certification as a secondary-school graduate.

The kind of mutually contradictory, pairwise statements, such as those of Fermat's experimental comparison of reflection and refraction of light, provide an example of the way in which a pre-existing ivory-tower form of mathematical physics often collapses when one attempts to extend it to previously unknown, or overlooked physical realities. The juxtaposing of a pair, or more, of such mutually contradictory statements, as formulated within some existing mathematical-physics doctrine, typifies an ontological paradox, as Plato, for example, addressed such phenomena. The juxtaposition of the contradictory elements of such an ontological paradox, typifies a statement in the form of *Analysis Situs*.

For example, in the history of arithmetic as such, there are ontological paradoxes among the notions of arithmetic, algebraic, and transcendental numbers. Plato addresses the first pair in his dialogues, and implies still higher cases, as in his *Timaeus*. These paradoxes and their implications, are addressed in one way by Kästner and his student Carl Gauss,[30] leading Gauss and his successors Lejeune Dirichlet and Riemann, to develop a new kind of mathematics and physics.[31] In

---

30. Carl Gauss, *Disquisitiones arithmeticae*. An 1889 German translation from the original Latin is available in a reprint edition: *Untersuchungen über höhere Arithmetik*, H. Maser, trans. (New York: Chelsea Publishing Co., 1981).

31. On Gauss, Dirichlet, and Riemann. Lazare Carnot and Alexander von Humboldt had been closely associated as members France's Ecole Polytechnique during the first decade of the Nineteenth Century. Humboldt continued an active relationship to the functioning of the Ecole, in Paris itself, until about 1827. During the interval following the Restoration monarchy's pro-British ouster of Monge and Carnot from the Ecole, Humboldt had worked both to maintain the Monge-Carnot legacy, and to build up Germany's science through support of the Monge-Carnot line of development of the Ecole in Germany. Dirichlet, one of Humboldt's leading protégés from the Ecole, moved to Berlin under Humboldt's patronage of both Gauss and Dirichlet. Dirichlet, a sometime teacher of Gauss protégé Riemann, succeeded Gauss in Göttingen, and Riemann then succeeded Dirichlet in that position. Notable features of the interconnections of the collaboration among Gauss, Dirichlet, and Riemann, are Riemann's emphasized reliance on what he termed "Dirichlet's Principle," and Riemann's superseding the work of Dirichlet, in continuing Dirichlet's correction of Euler's attempt to

The search for a solution to the ontological paradoxes posed by Kepler's and Fermat's discoveries, led, through the work of Gaspard Monge (left) et al., to the discovery and development of modern hypergeometry, by Carl Gauss (center) and Bernhard Riemann (right).

physical science as such, we discover two pertinent things about this. First, that all meaningful paradoxes introduced by higher categories of number, are phenomena which reflect some, underlying, corresponding function within physical science; and, second, that the existence of number itself originates in, and is controlled by the way in which the universe is organized according to physical principles, rather than the simply aprioristic notions of numerical ones, as the latter are typified by the assumptions of Bertrand Russell and such acolytes of his numerological cult as Norbert Wiener and John von Neumann.[32]

The first step in a well-organized process of discovery of some valid universal physical principle, is to define such an experimental quality of ontological paradox, by showing that the paradox must reflect a systemic flaw within (for example) the existing doctrines of mathematical physics as a whole. Such a paradox is stated most usefully in the form of a paradoxical statement in the form of *Analysis Situs*.

At that point in the investigation, the second step takes over. The ivory-tower pedant's classroom blackboard is banned from the continued proceedings, until an hypothetical solution is found. The solution to such a paradox will be found only in the domain of what is defined by Plato as *hypothesis*. This hypothesis must be in the form of a revolutionary change in the kind of mathematical physics used to state the paradox. This hypothesis has, and must have, the form and other quality demanded by the notion of a universal physical principle. Such an hypothesis is purely a creation of the sovereign cognitive powers of the individual mind of the thinker who generates that hypothesis. This is the most crucial fact about all valid methods of education, especially education for freedom.

The third step, once an hypothesis has been generated as a credible kind of proposed possible solution for the paradox, is to craft a design of experiment, which will test for two results. The first such result, must be to demonstrate that a real basis for the assumed effects of the hypothesis can be proven. The second result, must be to show that the hypothesis succeeds not only in some cases, but must be of the quality of *unique experiment* whose results can be regarded as a universal principle of any future mathematical physics.

If those conditions are satisfied, the solution to the paradox is apparently valid. The immediate next question posed is, therefore, how could the act of discovering and validating *the relevant hypothesis itself* be caused to occur in the mind of other persons? Now, we have touched the most essential question of all education. On the answer for this question, the very meaning of education itself depends entirely. *We have thus, now, reached the pivotal issue of our study of the subject of education as such.*

---

define a prime number series.

32. Bertrand Russell, *Principia Mathematica* (Cambridge: Cambridge University Press, 1994, reprint of 1927 edition). On this see Kurt Gödel on the fatal flaw in Russell's system: *On Formally Undecidable Propositions of Principia Mathematica and Related Systems* and *Discussion on Providing a Foundation for Mathematics*, **Collected Works,** Vol. I (New York: Oxford University Press, 1986).

EIRNS/Philip Ulanowsky

Physicist Dr. Robert Moon teaches a class on Ampère's discoveries in electromagnetism. "How could the act of discovering and validating the relevant hypothesis itself be caused to occur in the mind of other persons?"

We have a place. We have a date, or at least an approximate one. We have a name. We have relevant facts concerning his background, and his previous work. We have portraits which are putatively representations of Archimedes himself. We have a topographical and political map of the area of modern Italy and of the relevant portions of the Mediterranean, at the time the Sicilian Archimedes was about to be butchered by the invading Roman soldiers. We have also a general picture of the quality of Archimedes' accomplishments and of his relationship to the Eratosthenes, the world's greatest astronomer

Given two students within a class, who are given a statement of facts corresponding to an ontological paradox as I have described it above. Let each student withdraw from discussion with the teacher and other pupils for a time. Let each student attempt to solve the riddle, and put any proposed solution into the form of a plausibly arguable hypothesis.

That phase completed, let the class reassemble. Let each of the students who thinks he or she has discovered a solution for the riddle, now observe the teacher's demonstration of each among the students' proposed solutions. Assume that two among the students have solved the riddle, and that, therefore, the experimental demonstration shows that, at least, their proposed solutions are experimentally plausible. Now, the question becomes, which, if any, of those experimentally plausible solutions meet the standard of a universal physical principle?

Let us redefine that situation, as follows.

In this report so far, I have made reference to various celebrated discoverers and some part of their original discoveries. Now, instead of merely presenting the class with a riddle, let us make the subject of the riddle historically concrete, referencing one or more of those, or other discoverers. Let us take Archimedes' cry of "Eureka!" as the point of reference. What was Archi-

of that period, then living and working in Egypt, the latter a man of Cyrenaic origin, educated at Athens as a member of the Academy founded by Plato. Give the students the riddle of specific weight which Archimedes solved, by situating him as a real-life person in real history, in their minds, thus efficiently personalizing the task of replicating Archimedes' solution for the riddle. Don't give away the solution for the riddle, but, short of that, box the solution in, factually and historically, as much as possible otherwise.

This is the approach employed in a Classical humanist education.

Let us imagine the case in which two bright pupils, who have obviously been through similar experiences earlier, produce a plausible solution for the riddle. Then, after the demonstration experiment before the entire class, we have the following social situation.

The two relevant students from that class, have experienced a discovery of an hypothesis which is at least an approximation of Archimedes' success. Now, review the dramatis personae of the drama within the classroom as the demonstration is completed.

The teacher knows. Two of the students have each more or less replicated what happened within the sovereign cognitive processes of Archimedes; now that the demonstration experiment has been conducted, they are elated by the fact that they now really "see" the solution. The cry of "Eureka!" is now in order. Other pupils who have not solved the riddle, see a connection between the riddle and the demonstrated result of the discovery, and also see that fellow-students have been able to re-create a living moment from the mind of the great Archimedes within their own minds!

Meanwhile, inside the mind of each of the two students who produced fairly approximate hypothetical solutions for the riddle, there is a recognition of something of fundamental importance, *something uniquely human.*

There were three distinct, successive actions in the model case outlined. First, the paradox, then the hypothesis, and, finally, the validated discovery of principle which solves the paradox. It is the second of those three actions which is crucial: the act of *hypothesizing* a plausible, or entirely valid solution. Here lies the essential principle of all competent educational policy: the principle of cognitive hypothesizing of validatable discoveries of universal principle. Focus on the two successful students, and their state of mind in the aftermath of the demonstration and its discussion.

Focus on the fact that the relevant act of hypothesizing has occurred, independently, within the sovereign cognitive processes of each, a mental act whose occurrence is *intrinsically invisible* to sense-perception. Yet, that act of cognition was not only efficient action upon the real universe in which that event occurred, but, the application of the validated hypothesis to human practice will alter mankind's relationship to nature, a definite physical effect. The evidence generating the paradox was a matter of effects visible to the senses.

The concluding demonstration, was a matter of effects visible to the senses. However, the connection between the first and the last, however impassioned Archimedes' cry of "Eureka!" might be, is not "visible" to the senses. Therefore, how could the mind of John, one of those who replicated the experience of the discovery by Archimedes, "see" the thought of hypothesizing in the mind of the other student, Robert? Here, in this illustration, we have the germ of Plato's use of the term *idea.*

To the degree that John and Robert have experienced the act of hypothesizing in this case, they each have an experience which they know to be in correspondence with the relevant experience of the other. To that degree, Robert can "see" the act of hypothesizing within the mind of John, and vice versa. To avoid confusion in terms, let us, for the purpose of this report, call this not "synthetic judgment *a priori,*" but *Platonic insight.* Both can each see into that moment in the mind of the living Archimedes, in the same way. This cognitive connection among those three figures of this illustration, represents the germ of the truly human quality of social relations, and of the quality which sets the human individual, and species, apart from and above all other living species.

That is, of course, a very simple approximation of what an idea actually represents. Nonetheless, it is a good beginning; we shall improve upon it, step by step.

Plato's Cave

A close collaborator of both Gauss and Riemann, Wilhelm Weber, who was a gifted designer of scientific experimental apparatus, as well as a leading discoverer in the field of electromagnetism, made a very precise measurement, in connection with proving the Ampère angular-force principle, which was, in fact, the first successful modern intervention into sub-atomic microphysics.[33] It was also an idea produced as a part of the overthrow, as also by Ampère's collaboration with Fresnel and Arago, of not only the Newtonian doctrine of propagation of light, but also the general mathematical-physical dogma of the French Bourbon Restoration's "Newton freaks" Coulomb and Poisson.[34]

The advent of atomic, nuclear, and related microphysics, has the categorical experimental implication of showing that, at the very least, certain crucial sorts of sense-perception-observable macrophysical effects, are determined by efficient action located in a domain beyond direct access by human sense-perception.

Thus, Chicago University's Manhattan Project veteran, Professor Moon, speaking in support of the argument I had presented earlier, on the subject of controlled thermonuclear fusion, set before me his affirmative evidence for that same conclusion, that on one afternoon back during the mid-1970s. Moon explained to me (and, repeatedly to others among our collaborators),

33. Laurence Hecht, "The Atomic Science Textbooks Don't Teach: The Significance of the 1845 Gauss-Weber Correspondence," *21st Century Science & Technology,* Fall 1996; Jonathan Tennenbaum, "How Fresnel and Ampère Launched a Scientific Revolution," *EIR,* Aug. 27, 1999.
34. Laurence Hecht, "Should the Law of Gravity Be Repealed?," *21st Century Science & Technology,* Spring 2001; Jacques Cheminade, "The Ampère-Fresnel Revolution: 'On Behalf of the Future,'" *EIR,* Aug. 27, 1999.

that the work of Ampère-Weber et al., is evidence in support of ny insistence on the dubiousness of the assumption, that the purely arbitrary presumption, that repulsive "Coulomb forces" are extended simply infinitely, into large and small, is only arbitrary, and not very intelligent, ivory-tower speculation, rather than sound physics. This proof, as set forth by Professor Moon, of the absurdity of such taught dogma as the so-called "Coulomb" principle, exposes the folly of the presumption by some, that a "Coulomb barrier" constitutes a principled barrier to any development of controlled thermonuclear fusion power production for society.[35]

This brings us directly to the crucial topic of "Plato's Cave." Plato's pedagogical allegory was, that what our senses present to us, must be assessed as analogous to the shadows appearing on the irregular surface of the wall of a dimly-lit cave, rather than the objects responsible for that projection of those shadows. Microphysics is an obvious case of such an *ontologically paradoxical quality* of sense-perception.

However, the rule is, that the basis for Plato's argument is not the absurd argument of the bogomils and also the empiricists such as Locke, Bernard Mandeville, François Quesnay, and Adam Smith, that unseeable little demons, whether called "invisible hands," or "Maxwell's demons,"[36] are the prompters of visible effects. The crucial point is, that each and every discovery of an experimentally validatable universal physical principle, shows that the universe is not controlled by aprioristic kinds of statistical principles; it is controlled, essentially, as Kepler discovered the universal principle of gravitation, by those objects of cognition which we know, as my story's John and Robert did, as the kinds of *ideas* associated with the human *act* of making such discoveries. In physical science, such *ideas* are otherwise known by the name of experimentally validated universal physical principles.[37]

These are *ideas* in the sense indicated by the way in which Robert is able to look insightfully into the mind of John, in the case of the shared cognitive experience of discovering an experimentally validated universal physical principle.

This connotes, that our sense-perception is not merely something as trivial, and false, as a faithful image of the real universe, but presents us with the mere shadows of physical reality. It is the business of the mind, as the mind is typified by the cognitive action, which generates validated discoveries of universal physical principle, in response to ontological paradoxes. It is the business of the mind, acting in this cognitive way, to discover the reality which corresponds to the effects projected upon our sensorium.

At this point, I summarize the relevant elements of an argument made, with included reference to the work of the founder of the branch of science known as *bio-geochemistry*, Vladimir I. Vernadsky, in earlier published locations.

Vernadsky divided the phenomena experienced in the universe among three categories of what he termed *natural objects*.[38] The first is the category of natural ob-

---

35. My own argument had been the much more modest argument, that it was fraudulent to presume that a Newtonian conception, such as that of so-called "Coulomb forces," could be neither arbitrarily extended into the "infinitely small" and "infinitely large," nor assumed to be linear. I had argued, as a matter of our policy, that the matter of "forces at work" on the scale of the nuclear fusion must be left to relevant experimental work. Thus, until Moon's presentation of the crucial implications of the Ampère-Weber principle, our policy had been based on those negative considerations or principle alone; Moon gave us the positive basis needed for the policies respecting controlled nuclear fusion, then formulated on behalf of what, soon after that, became the Fusion Energy Foundation. In 1986, Dr. Moon proposed a model of the atomic nucleus, based on a study of Kepler's work on the Solar system, in which the protons occupy the vertex positions of nested shells of four of the five Platonic solids.

36. The Massachusetts Institute of Technology's Professor Norbert Wiener, premised the core of his argument for the founding of the irrationalist cult of so-called "information theory," on citing J. Clerk Maxwell's speculation, that phenomena such as "negative entropy" could be explained by assuming the presence of an invisible little "demon" operating within the cracks of the infinitesimally small. Although this is the same argument made, for theology, by the neo-manichean cult known as the bogomils, and, explicitly, in support of "free trade," by Bernard Mandeville, François Quesnay, and Adam Smith, Wiener's citation of Maxwell reflects Wiener's and John von Neumann's conditioning as one-time acolytes of Bertrand Russell. This doctrine, shared by the latter two, provided the basis for the 1970s development of the "Third Wave" cult of Newt Gingrich, Alvin Toffler, Al Gore, et al., and it also supplies the supernatural doctrine of "The New Economy" derived from that "Third Wave" cult.

37. The formal denial of the existence of universal physical principles, so defined, is traced to the famous series of *Critiques* of Immanuel Kant. Modern cult-doctrines of "information theory" and "artificial intelligence" are radical derivatives of the argument, against knowable discoveries of universal physical principles, first published by Kant in his ***Critique of Pure Reason*** (Garden City, N.Y.: Doubleday & Company, Inc., 1966, translation of 1781 edition). That argument is used by neo-Kantians, such as the positivist followers of Ernst Mach, Boltzmann, et al., as the premise for efforts to reduce the mathematical practice of science to linear statistical methods of the so-called "radical empiricists," as the devotees of Wiener and von Neumann do.

38. Vladimir I. Vernadsky, "On the Fundamental Material-energetic Difference between Living and Non-Living Natural Bodies in the Bio-

jects of non-living processes, the second of living processes (the *biosphere*), and the third of cognitive (*noëtic*) processes. In each case, the distinct difference of these types of natural objects, within the overlapping action among the classes, is defined empirically by the evidence of the changes which living processes successfully impose upon non-living ones (such as the body of natural objects constituting the *biosphere*), and the higher order of changes which human cognitive processes impose upon the functions of the biosphere (the *noösphere)*.

Since these differences are measured as the natural effects of those physical principles as causes, they are called by Vernadsky *natural objects*. Physical science is properly defined as the discovery of the principles expressed in the form of the process of production of such natural objects. The differences in effects of action among such classes of objects, such as the distinction between non-living and living, cognitive and non-cognitive, are measured in terms of the successively higher orders of *anti-entropy* characteristic of that succession, and are properly defined as of the quality of universal physical principles. This definition, as described by Vernadsky, among others, is based upon the experimental evidence of the corresponding uniqueness of the physical effects associated uniquely with each category of action.[39]

Within each of those three general types of ideas, there are experimentally defined, distinct ideas of valid universal physical principles. My discoveries in the field of the science of physical economy, have the effect of being an insertion into the internal features of the cognitive functions defining the *noösphere* as man's successful transformation of the biosphere, a biosphere which, in turn, is transforming the non-living processes of our planet by such means as creating oceans and atmosphere.

My own original discoveries in the field of physical economy, were prompted by attention to the role of technological progress in increasing the implied power of mankind to exist in our universe, as this could be measured per capita, and per square kilometer of normalized surface-area of Earth. I recognized this as a reflection of the same principle of *anti-entropy*[40] which leading biologists had recognized as the characteristic, marginal mathematical distinction of living processes from non-living ones.[41] My discoveries along that line of inquiry, led, in turn, to my subsequent recognition of both the importance of Riemann for interpreting the application of my discoveries, and the importance of Vernadsky's discoveries for situating the result within the universe at large.

The idea of such measurements had been prompted, in large part, by my adolescent studies of the work of Leibniz, in which his notions of physical economy, as he developed those notions over the course of the 1671-1716 interval, radiate from the pores of his work in general. The essential feature of Leibniz's work reflected in my own attack on the problem of physical economy, was Leibniz's notion of a *monadology*.

There are in the universe, objects such as planetary orbits, as Kepler was the first known to us to define the meaning of a planetary orbit as a *cognitively* distinct object. It was Leibniz's continuation of the combined work of Kepler, and of Fermat on "quickest-action pathway," which led to both Leibniz's uniquely original discovery of the calculus, and, thence, beyond the calculus as such, to those principles of physical science set forth as his monadology.

The effect of the orbit is always distinct, as Kepler showed the harmonic ordering of relative values among

---

sphere" (1938), Jonathan Tennenbaum and Rachel Douglas, trans., *21st Century Science & Technology*, Winter 2000-2001.
39. This is in opposition to the quietly hysterical reference, implicitly against Vernadsky, to so-called "aperiodic crystals," in the "What Is Life?" essay by Boltzmann follower Erwin Schrödinger. Schrödinger hysterically avoids the fallacy of composition underlying his own argument, that the Clausius-Grassmann-Kelvin notion of entropy is a product not of physical science, but of the hereditary implications of the a priori assumptions of Boltzmann's mathematics.

40. My use of "anti-entropy" parallels Kästner's use of the term "anti-Euclidean geometry," and Gauss's and Riemann's following Kästner's teaching of this principle. I was, however reluctantly, obliged to abandon the use of "negative entropy," which had had an excellent record in the field of biology earlier, because of the massive propaganda in support of Bertrand Russell acolyte Norbert Wiener's vulgarization of the term "negative entropy."
41. This is not to argue that the non-living aspects of the universe are characteristically entropic, but only that there exists a characteristic margin of *relative* anti-entropy, distinguishing living processes from non-living ones of comparable chemical composition. The notion of universal thermodynamical entropy, as associated with the reading of the work of Clausius, Grassmann, and Kelvin, is derived from a dubious imposition of a radically reductionist set of axioms upon the model of the work of Sadi Carnot. The resulting mathematical notion of a universal principle of kinematic entropy is, from its inception, an hereditary implication of the dubious axioms pre-embedded in the mathematics applied to the study. The resulting error is a faithful copy of the common, fatal blunder of ivory-tower mathematics, which Kepler exposed in the cases of Claudius Ptolemy, Copernicus, and Brahe.

Johannes Kepler (left) was the first known to us to define the meaning of a planetary orbit as a cognitively distinct object. Gottfried Leibniz (right) took up where Kepler left off, leading to his uniquely original discovery of the calculus.

the planetary orbits; the caused effect is always a definitely measurable one, but the cause of that effect can not be simply reduced, on principle, to the same exact (constant) form of simple numbers under all circumstances in general. Put most simply, anything which exists, is interacting with larger processes. It is not only interacting with other processes, but is acting within, and acted upon by a manifold expressing the universal physical geometry within which all of these processes are situated, and by which they are controlled. The role of harmonics for Kepler, in determining the relations among the planetary orbits, expresses this principle.

Therefore, in considering any such subject, we must distinguish between the notion of its existence as an existence, and the relative value that existence expresses within a relevant physical-space-time geometry, such as a Riemannian hypergeometry.

I emphasize, that we must not limit our attention to pairwise interaction among other systems of events; we must recognize the efficient principle of action represented by the physical manifold as such, within which all apparently pairwise interactions occur. In other words, we must adduce the notion of a specific physical space-time (hypergeometrical) "curvature," not only as a physically efficient form of action upon all within it, but as a curvature upon which the individual action is itself acting, as if reciprocally. This is implicit in Ke-

pler's discoveries, but becomes explicit only through the work of such followers of Leibniz as Gauss and Riemann. An object so situated and defined, is what Leibniz signifies by the term *monad.*

On the condition that we define objects from the standpoint of cognition, rather than naive sense-certainty, we have, as Leibniz emphasized, a vast plenum of such objects, and also categories of objects. For example, there are the relatively simpler objects of non-living processes, also planetary systems, living processes, and the cognitive processes of the individual person. Each belongs to the class of monads, but each belongs to a distinct class, and is distinct within its class. Each has an identity as a non-Aristotelean form of existence, and also a definable, relative notion of the measurable, relative, non-Aristotelean characteristics of the action associated with that existence.

All such monads are associated with the notion of a Platonic idea, ideas akin to the relatively successful mental (cognitive) act of hypothesizing by our John and Robert. It is as such *ideas*, that the applicable meaning of the term monad is to be defined.

Our knowledge of such ideas is essentially practical in form. *The discovery of any valid universal physical principle, typifies the sole means by which a characteristic increase in man's power to exist within the universe is effected.* By that, we should understand man's increased *(anti-entropic)* power to exist, as a species, into an indefinite number of future generations, as improvement of this existence can be measured per capita and per square kilometer of surface area. That consideration is the primary experimental basis for any science of physical economy.

The shaping of the physical-economic policies of a society, to bring about that combined result, for the benefit of both present and, especially, future mankind, is of a quality which I have defined, in earlier locations, as a scientific intention, following Kepler's use of *Mind* and *intention* as synonyms for efficient forms of universal physical principles. Physical economy is the science of physical intentions, as these are to be embedded in a nation's laws and related policies, for the increase of mankind's per-capita potential relative population-density into a generation ahead, and beyond.

In the rather common case, the design of a successful experiment which proves the validity of an hypothetical universal physical principle, must contain, by its nature, as if hereditarily, some included feature of design which corresponds to the principle being tested. The application of the results of such a feature of such an experiment, to the designs of products and processes, for example, is a result which we recognize as a *technology.*

It is the knowledgeable application of science and technology, so defined, to man's action on the universe, per capita and per square kilometer, which is the determining basis for the physically defined productive powers of labor. Thus, the higher the level of educational development of the person, through related cognitive experiences, the relatively higher the *relative* productive powers of labor of that quality.[42]

That point restated: the combination of the level of development and maintenance of the basic economic infrastructure of the general area and the conditions of the general population, with the levels of knowledge practiced in design and production of useful products, expresses a relationship between the characteristic curvature of that society considered as a Riemannian sort of physical space-time, and the act of production or consumption within that space-time setting. The relative value of a productive act, lies not merely in the internal quality of the intention expressed by that act, but the relative "curvature" of the physical space-time represented by the physical economy in which that act occurs.

Here so far, we have considered only those ideas which are associated with conventional notions of the subject of physical science. This brings us to the third consideration identified above: the social process.

Human Relations

In his work founding modern experimental physical science, *De Docta Ignorantia*, Nicholas of Cusa included report of his work correcting an error by Archimedes, in the matter of the quadrature of the circle (and, implicitly, the parabola). Cusa's report on that matter is the original discovery of a class of geometric numbers subsequently known as *transcendental.*[43] The further implications of this line of development, as to mathematics generally, were broadly settled by the continuing work of Gauss on the implications of bi-quadratic residues.

This case implicitly puts us into the middle of a process of the unfolding of the development of a plenum of cognitive ideas, from Thales and Pythagoras, through Plato, Eratosthenes, Archimedes, Cusa, Kepler, Leibniz, Gauss, and Riemann, and also including all the ideas implied in that succession of discovery. In any competent program of secondary and higher education, the pupils have, like the students John and Robert of our story, relived the cognitive act of original discovery of some of the crucial discoveries of universal physical principle, by each and all of these and comparable historical figures of scientific progress.

Moreover, these ideas are not ideas which exist in isolation from one another; there is a qualitative interdependency of the existence of the discovery of any idea, upon the situation presented by the accumulation of an ultimately enormous array of actual, or merely alleged cognitive discoveries of principle by predecessors. Some years ago, in a featured article, I compared such an array of predecessors to the historical figures assembled by Raphael Sanzio in his *The School of Athens.*[44]

Focus upon that historical class of ideas as subjects of the replication of the cognitive act of the historically original discovery, rather than merely learning. Compare the cognitive relationship to these discoverers, of any student who has successfully relived the experience of discovering those principles, principles known to the student by the name and historical setting of each of those earlier discoverers. Compare the relationship

---

42. This is also relative to the level of development of basic economic infrastructure. Labor of equal skill, situated in a relatively poorer general level of development of basic economic infrastructure, will be of poor quality in its result, even catastrophically so. As I defined the point in earlier locations, basic economic infrastructure is to be seen as a part of the function of the biosphere, as the quality of that biosphere has been enriched with natural products of cognitive activity, such as products of science and technology.

43. Although, it should be clear that this is already implied in the treatment of the Plato Academy's proof of the uniqueness of the Platonic solids, as reflected and elaborated within Plato's *Timaeus,* and as this feature of the work of Cusa, Pacioli, and Leonardo occupies a central place in the work of Kepler.

44. Lyndon H. LaRouche, Jr., "The Truth About Temporal Eternity," *Fidelio,* Summer 1994.

Raphael's *"The School of Athens."*

of the student to each of those discoverers to the relationship among John, Robert, and Archimedes, in the illustration provided above.

Look at Raphael's ***School of Athens***. I propose that the reader work through the following exercise.

Make a list of each of the historical figures represented. Take a map of the relevant area of the Mediterranean and its littoral for the period from the time of Homer through the entirety of the Classical and Hellenistic phases of Greek and related culture. Locate the place and date of existence of each figure on that map. Then, identify the relationship among these figures in terms of those leading ideas which bear upon the irreconcilable dispute between the cognitive Plato and his opponent, the reductionist Aristotle. Ask yourself, is the gloomy figure in the foreground, perhaps the Classical Platonist Raphael's recognition of the Romantic tendencies in his contemporary, Michelangelo?

In this collection as a whole, there are sequences of time, and sequences of ideas, or beliefs, such as Aristotle's, substituted for ideas. In the painting, these figures are represented as contemporaries, as if the entire period represented by these figures' mortal lives, had been compacted into a kind of simultaneity of eternity.

Yet, when one considers the medley of interacting ideas and other beliefs represented by the whole assembly, there is an order defined in terms of action among both kinds of notions treated as principles by the user, either ideas or substitutes for ideas, or a combination of both.

Ask: What is the meaning of Raphael's resort to such a portrayal of a simultaneity of eternity? Is it not the case, that that painting corresponds to the way in which a well-educated student's mind, even a graduate of a decent sort of secondary education, sees such figures from that period of history? His mind is a simultaneity of eternity, but there is also an ordering, in the sense of sequences, among the elements of that otherwise timeless eternity.

In other words, by introducing the notion of *change as such*, in the form of continuing, superseding generation of ideas, the time during which the changes unfold is collapsed into a relatively very short lapse of time within the bounds of what is otherwise a simultaneity of eternity.

Now, amplify this memory of history, to include virtually all that pertains to physical scientific knowledge, and to the known aspects of the history of cultures, and of the geography in which they dwelt. We will have then amplified Raphael's example, to approximate the functional elements of the memory of ideas by a well-educated individual mind of today. If that memory is organized around the efficient interaction among ideas defined in Platonic terms, we have imagined thus, the case which I wish to call to your attention here.

The relationship of the students John and Robert to Archimedes, in my pedagogical story, is to be recognized as an expression of the truly essential nature of human relations *per se*, as distinct from the quality of relationship among lower forms of animal life (as mimicked by such as the empiricist devotees of Hobbes, Locke, Mandeville, Quesnay, Adam Smith, Jeremy Bentham, and Bertrand Russell, implicitly profess themselves to be). *Truly human relations, are expressed as relations in terms of a Platonic notion of ideas.*

To emphasize the crucial point here, when we shift the notion of events, from mere sense-experiences as such, to the development of ideas, everything believed about the nature of experience changes accordingly. We then contrast the relative clock-time associated with sense-experience as such, to the relative time expressed by the rate of progress in ideas, that relative to whatever physical process we are measuring in terms of rate of progress. We shift the notion of human relations, from the sensuality of mortal sense-experience, to the passion of the universe of cognitive transmission of development of ideas.[45]

Pause at this point, to reflect on the importance of naming discoverers, of naming the time and place in history in which each discovery is believed to have occurred for the first time. There is an essential function which requires naming ideas in that historical way, rather than the way in which the worst among today's textbooks and classroom instruction tend to do. As my story of John and Robert illustrates the point, *the most essential feature of all ideas, is the historical relationship expressed in the communication of those ideas in the cognitive form they assumed as hypothesis.*

This is the most essential principle of all competent educational policy of practice, as the Friedrich Schiller-Wilhelm von Humboldt program of Classical-humanist education typifies such competence.[46] Without that notion of the historically determined, functional relations among the discoveries and rediscoveries of ideas in their Platonic form, no scientific rigor can be achieved; worse, no rational comprehension of the existence of society is possible.

The way in which societies, such as the U.S. today, degrade the personalities of their individual members into an Orwellian condition like that of human cattle, is through the substitution of popular opinion, as Romantic tradition and Walter Lippmann have defined it, for truth. To this end, explanations of the type often referred to today as "spin," and outright, especially official and academic lies, as well as wicked fables and mythologies, are supplied to the credulous as a substitute for knowledge. The case of so-called "religious fundamentalist" beliefs, is among the best examples of the way official and quasi-official, lying mythologies, are used to control the minds and behavior of large strata of populations, "Big Brother" fashion.[47] Any well-edu-

---

45. It was the inherent inability of a thorough Aristotelean, such as Padua's Pietro Pomponazzi, to accept that distinction, which impelled him, and all of like persuasion, such as the empiricists, to see human existence in any but strictly *mortalist* terms. Only in the realm of cognitive processes, which, like life as such, does not exist in Aristotle's system of only animal life, of *anima*, does the mortal individual have an efficiently continuing relationship to a pre- and post-mortal past and future. Hence, the Christian, in contrast to Pomponazzi, makes a distinction between the mortal being and the cognitive being made in the image of the Creator, the soul.

46. Friedrich Schiller wrote his seminal piece on education, *Letters on the Aesthetical Education of Man*, during the several months in Jena, Germany, beginning in 1794, when he was in the almost daily company of Wilhelm von Humboldt. Schiller's **On Grace and Dignity,** begun in May 1793, is his first major published work to decisively criticize the perspective of Kant on aesthetics. Schiller's inaugural lecture at Jena University, "What Is, and to What End Do We Study, Universal History," delivered on May 26-27, 1789, shows what Schiller's philosophy was, as a teacher.

Von Humboldt captures Schiller's impact, in his essay "On Schiller and the Course of His Spiritual Development" (1830). Von Humboldt was appointed Privy Councillor and director of the Section for Ecclesiastical Affairs and Education in the Ministry of the Interior of Prussia in 1808, and remained there for 16 months. Two key memoranda, produced in this period, outline his philosophy of education: the "school plans" for Königsberg and Prussian Lithuania. Humboldt's ideas were put into practice in Prussia during his ministry, and continued to influence German education until the 1970s "reforms" of Willy Brandt's government. The founding of the University of Berlin, beginning in September 1807, was Humboldt's crowning achievement.

All the writings by Schiller and Humboldt referenced here are available in English translation from the Schiller Institute (www.schillerinstitute. org).

47. There should be standards, akin to "pure food" criteria, or labels warning credulous consumers, against the acceptance of the claims of many curious sects, such as those of Rev. Pat Robertson and Jerry Falwell, to the name of "Christianity." The crucial feature of the latter variety of pseudo-Christian cults, is that they claim that "God's intention is to be found in an ordinary individual's reading of the text of passages from the Bible," a variety of the same argument made by the wildly gnostic, self-avowed "textualist," U.S. Supreme Court Associate Justice

Friedrich Schiller (left) and Wilhelm von Humboldt. Their program of Classical-humanist education typifies the essential principle of competent educational policy: the communication of the history of ideas in their cognitive form.

The emphasis should be on the word "intent." The instant one challenges a fraudulent myth of academia, the banshees are unleashed against the offender. Pedants of what ordinarily appear to be of a mind most successfully detached from reality, fly into a mentally deranged state of rage against the violator of what passes for "the code." The phrase from Eugene O'Neill's *The Iceman Cometh* pops into mind: "Hickey, you took the life out of the booze!" Once the hypnotic spell of accepted mythology is broken, as by the mere mention of an embarrassing bit of truth, the enraged reaction to this from the thoroughly conditioned pedant, betrays the fact that the dogma being defended by the pedant is a device concocted to serve, and be enforced as a control mechanism over the minds of the credulous members of the student population. You are the target of his, or her rage, because you have unmasked the magician, and spoiled his magic: you have taken the life out of the booze he was intentionally dispensing for its intended effects.

cated person in study of history, recognizes the way in which synthetic religions and other mythologies have been used, as a principal method of effectively dictatorial control over large portions, even the virtual entirety of entire populations, even entire cultures.[48] Much of what passes for education in science and other matters, in today's universities and public schools, is of this degraded nature and wicked intent.[49]

The essence of what we should recognize today as Orwellian brainwashing of large populations for purposes set forth in Fabian ideologue Walter Lippmann's 1922 *Public Opinion*, is the total substitution of the claimed authority of arbitrary forms of mere *belief* for knowledge. I described such substitution of mere belief for knowledge, in my references, earlier in this report, to the kind of lying which I encountered as dominating opinion among family and school environments during my childhood and adolescence. The use of the modern

Antonin Scalia. Typical of the point to be made, is the absurdity of any attempt to apply the "textualist" practice to *I Corinthians* 13, in which the Apostle Paul defines the meaning of Plato's conception of *agapē* according to a most essential Christian principle. Notably, the type of "Biblical fundamentalist" referenced has no agreement with the literal intent of such authorities as the Apostles John and Paul. Indeed, all such "fundamentalist" doctrines are the clearest examples of wild varieties of anti-Christian gnosticism, with clear affinities for the doctrine of the anti-Christian bogomil cult.

48. Thus, a nation can be truly a democracy and also truly a dictatorship exerted by an oligarchy. Such is the nature of the degeneration of the U.S.A., especially since Richard Nixon's launching of his 1966-1968 campaign for the Presidency. The degeneration of the character of political parties as organizations of the citizenry, into a master-client relationship, instead, typifies the role of a pro-"Southern Strategy"-oriented, oligarchy-controlled mass media, in crushing the U.S. population into a condition of rule by "popular opinion," a condition akin to the status of the lower classes, plebeians, and slaves, of ancient Rome.

49. It is very much to the credit of author James D. Anderson, that, in the 1988 book I have referenced here, he stresses the conscious intention of Wall Street banker George F. Peabody, 1914 Woodrow Wilson appointee as Vice-Chairman of the New York Federal Reserve Bank, as

typical of those who controlled much of so-called "black education" in the U.S.A. as an intended control mechanism directed immediately against the so-called African-American population. The same methods were used, by interests of the same Wall Street pedigree, to introduce into public schools and universities, mythologies intended to terminate the role of the ideas represented by Rev. Martin Luther King among so-called African-Americans, as in some propagandistic efforts to discredit the memory of Frederick Douglass.

mass media, notably an entertainment and news media which can no longer be strictly distinguished from one another, to orchestrate a synthetic *vox populi* better named *vox pox*, is exemplary of what we may recognize as the functions of the use of myths and fables for mass social control in former history.

The question posed by today's Orwellian practices to such effect, is, how could a population defend itself against control by the kind of mass-media and related methods of mind-manipulation rampant in the U.S.A. today?

The relevant difference between myth and truth, credulity and reason, is located in the way in which human relations are defined.

If the student has experienced each ancient and other discovery of validated universal physical principle, by means of reliving the historically situated act of original discovery of that principle, the student now knows personally that moment in the mind of the living original discoverer of relevance. There lies the pivotal distinction.

However, competent scientific knowledge is not a mere basketful of separately collected discoveries from the past. Usually, as in the case of the combined impact of the cognitively referenced discoveries by Kepler and Fermat, upon the minds and work of Christiaan Huyghens, Leibniz, et al., the Leibniz calculus, for example, was developed. Knowledge of universal principles, gained in this way, is a highly reticulated, highly inter-dependent lattice-work of an historical, ongoing process of continuing discovery and rediscovery of ideas of a Platonic form. We should say, that this is a multiply-connected lattice-work, as Riemann signifies by his use of "multiply-connected." The process of knowledge is an organic process, rooted in the principle of cognitive action.

A competent process of education, is organized and conducted according to that conception of the cognitive experiencing of the relevant lattice-work of validated discoveries of universal physical principles, up to the present time. That goal is accomplished, by limiting the core of all educational practices and related experiences, to the experiencing of the cognitive process of generating knowledge, rather than by means of learning. *The primary intent of any good education, is to produce a graduate who embodies the most essential achievements of history, in that way, up to that moment.*

"The primary intent of any good education, is to produce a graduate who embodies the most essential achievements of history … up to that moment"—a goal to which this young man apparently aspires.

3. 'Science and Culture'

A good education does not end with the subject of the discovery and application of universal physical principles as such. Although we must measure economic performance, and its demographic characteristics, in physical terms, and per capita and per square kilometer of a normalized cross-section of the Earth's surface, the individual does not act solely as an individual, but also as a product of, and functioning part of an entire society. When we consider a society's relationship to the planet on which it lives, it is the ordering of the social relations within the society, which determines the ability of the society to cooperate in ways which make the fostering of discovery of universal principles, and their application, effective, if they are to become, indeed, truly effective.

Stated in terms of the implications of a Riemannian physical geometry, the productive potential of the individual lies not entirely within himself, but in the relationship of his development to the characteristic "curvature" of the society and more immediate circumstances in which his function is situated.

This brings us, now, to the second principal aspect of a competent form of education, the role of Classical culture in determining the relative ability of a society to discover, and to utilize knowledge of validated universal physical principles.

The best way in which to define this second aspect of a Classical humanist education, is to focus, first, on the role of what is strictly definable as a Classical humanist species of artistic culture, as this is distinct from, and also the natural adversary of either Romantic forms of culture, or those so-called popular, modernist, and post-modernist novelties which a jaded Romanticism has concocted, apparently, at least in part, in its desire to escape from its boredom with its tedious self.

Situate what I have said in this report so far, in terms of the referenced discoveries reported by Vernadsky. See the place of human relations within a functional image of what Vernadsky defines as the noösphere.

In Vernadsky's imagery, we have three classes of what I have defined in this report as *experimentally validated universal physical principles*. I restate that argument now:

The first, is a set of such principles as might be assumed to be acting within and upon a non-living universe.

The second, is what Vernadsky defined as the *biosphere*, a principle of life, not derived from the physics of non-living processes, which is able to impose its *intention*, as Kepler uses the notion of "intention," to place the Earth under increasing domination of the effects of action by a principle of life as such, thus producing a *biosphere*.

The third, is the power of willful, cognitive ("noëtic") discovery, unique to the human species, by which mankind is able to impose its will to change the characteristic behavior of both non-living processes in general, and of the effects of the principle of life in general. This creates the *noösphere*.

These three classes of experimentally validated knowledge of universal physical principle, represent, combined, an implicitly Riemannian form of multiply-connected manifold of three distinct types of universal physical principles.

In the study of the efficient role of cognition within the context of the noösphere so conceived, what are those physically efficient forms of relations which define the cooperation upon which man's efficient role within the noösphere depends?

As is reflected most explicitly in the science of physical economy, the ultimate validation of the hypothetical principles governing efficient forms of cognitive relations among the members of society, lies in manifest physical effects produced, or what Vernadsky's argument defines as the natural products of cognitive ("noëtic") activity. That natural product is the increase of the potential relative population-density of the society, or human species as a whole. Since cause and effect express themselves over generations, this subject must be considered over a span of not less than several successive generations. Those changes in the organization of society and its physical economy, which determine such increases, represent the natural products of cognition, as defined in the way consistent with the way in which Vernadsky uses his general notion of natural products.

Thus, the view of a natural science of culture defined by the principle of the sovereign cognitive process of the individual mind, requires that we adduce the principles underlying cognitive relations within society, by a study of the relative superiority or inferiority of forms of culture, as adduced from long-range studies of those changes in culture which are empirically the most characteristic, relative features of multi-generational trends of change within the evolution of society in general.

Since the changes in culture introduced by the revolutionary establishment of the first modern sovereign form of nation-state, during Europe's Fifteenth Century, is, as measured by the standard of potential relative population-density, by far the most successful development in human culture known, we must proceed from a study of the relevant qualities of changes which that revolution has introduced to the preceding phases of both ancient and medieval European civilization. At the same time, we must focus upon those conflicts within European civilization which show us which cultural trends within modern European civilization are responsible for the improvements, and which, as Henry C. Carey showed for the case of slavery, detrimental in their effects upon the society's development as a whole.

In the later sections of the present section of this report, I shall emphasize those issues to be seen from the standpoint of the role of Classical humanist policies of education, in the struggle against slavery and its effects within the U.S.A. itself. In the subsequent section, I shall turn to the role of today's globally extended modern European civilization within the economy and culture of humanity as a whole.

Thus, we continue this section of the report, by beginning now with a restatement of an immediately crucial point.

Where mankind's discovery of universal physical principles of non-living and living processes as such, deals with the relationship of the individual human mind to the universe, the ability of the human species to accumulate, transmit, and use such knowledge, depends upon discovery of certain universal principles of the human mind, principles upon which society depends for the successful application of what are physical principles of nature, as the latter are considered apart from viewing the problems of individual and society in terms of the measurable effects of mankind's relationship to the universe at large. We must distinguish between the potential relative population-density of society, as measured from the standpoint of the physical universe outside us, and the manner in which society organizes its internal, social relations, to produce changes in society's voluntary relationship to the physical universe.

This involves a crucial point, and must be made clear, even if it costs a bit more effort to do so.

In the usages of Vernadsky, the effective increase of the potential relative population-density of mankind is a *natural product* of a cognition-driven progress in the practice of society, upon the biosphere which it inhabits. This is the form in which physical productivity of society can be measured for its relative success in improving its ability to exist in terms of the world around it.

The making of that natural product, occurs within a different dimension of the process. It occurs primarily as the cognitive production of valid discoveries (or enactments of discoveries) of universal physical principles; but, the fostering of those discoveries and their application, is a reflection of a social process, the process in which mankind defines relations within society.

So, those social processes, especially the social processes associated with the transmission and application of ideas as ideas, are themselves properly the subject of the same methods of investigation used for discovering universal physical principles in the domains of non-living and living processes in general.

To restate that point, we have the following. The cognitive work of scientific discovery must be continued, from the subject of mankind's effective physical relationship to the universe at large, to the subject of the principles governing the way in which man's ability to cooperate for the mastery of nature, is determined in terms of the relations among the cognitive processes of the individual members of society at large. Just as mankind must discover how better to order our species' physical relationship to the universe, the noösphere, in which we live, we must discover those principles needed to better order such task-oriented relations among ourselves.

This signifies that our programs of education, and related activities, must rise above the application of cognition to the narrower purpose of discovery of valid universal physical principles respecting man's direct mastery of the non-living universe and biosphere. We must broaden the inquiry, to focus upon the application of cognition to the discovery of the universal principles governing the efficient consequences of relevant, directly functional relations among the cognitive processes of persons. We must, so to speak, expand upon what is demonstrated as the cognitive relationship among the minds of John, Robert, and Archimedes, to include the generality of such cognitive relations within society.

This application of the principle of cognition to the subject of the functions of the cognitive relations within society, is best named *Classical humanist culture*. The clue leading to solutions to this problem, is study of the way in which self-conscious forms of cognitively creative social behavior in children, determine the possibility of healthy forms of functioning of adult society, or, in the alternative, how the lack of such cognitive development among the young, tends toward descent of the adult society into bestiality. The theme of such an inquiry, must be the subject of policies of education.

The essence of all competent forms of Classical artistic composition, is *the principle of cognitive play*. For example, the person who is not more or less effervescent in impulses for specifically cognitive forms of playfulness, as Wolfgang Mozart expresses that quality so beautifully, or J.S. Bach before him, has little or no capacity for sustained creative work in general, either scientific, or in Classical forms of artistic composition and performance in particular.

I have suggested, in earlier locations, that one might examine more closely the happier instances of play between a boy and his puppy, noting particularly the impulse of the mentally healthy boy for invention of harmless games, which the puppy then happily learns. In that combined symbiosis and difference between boy and

<UNICEF/Ray Witlin>

"The essence of all competent forms of Classical artistic composition, is the principle of cognitive play." Here: a day-care center in Bolivia.

beast, a principle of humanism is being demonstrated. Nicholas of Cusa, on this account, referenced the animal's participation in man, as parallelling man's participation in God the Creator. The morally healthy order among living creatures, is the participation of the lower species in the work of the higher.[50]

Perhaps the best way to describe the individual's impulse for cognitive play, is to regard this as the individual's impulse, at least implicitly so, to play with the Creator, as the puppy desires to play with a boy who treats it well. I think that neither Cusa nor Friedrich Schiller would disagree with that. Plato's Socrates is a paradigm for such a playful individual; the dialogues are models of a quality of play which seeks to define forms of behavior which are cognitively pleasing, not only because of the need of the sane human individual

to be cognitive, but the desire to choose games in which nothing sordid or unjust ensues.

The characteristic of such cognitive play, is the exercise and development of the powers of cognition themselves. This may be expressed, in approximation, either as the development of the individual powers to rally one's mental powers for making discoveries, which might be termed developing one's cognitive mental muscles, or may emphasize the specific capacities needed for cognitive undertakings in direct, explicitly cognitive modes of cooperation with others.

The study of these matters, from that standpoint, obliges us to focus attention on the relationship between productive forms of play in young children and the productive role of the more developed forms of play which are essential to the best performance of adults. The study of that connection is the proper definition of education.

Classical Drama As Science

So, ironically, but also insightfully, we also use the word "play" to describe what we may regard as a successful design for a drama. In the emergence of what became known as Classical Greece, the successive emergence of the Homeric epics, the Classical tragedy, and the Socratic dialogues of Plato, represent phases of development, in that form, of what is meaningfully identified as a notion of a Classical artistic principle of composition and performance for today.

From the *New Testament*, we have the parable of the *talents*. The impulse for cognitive play, is the talent which must be returned to the Creator enriched by the user. In other words, play as the work of generating anti-entropy for the sake of humanity. In what is called physical science and the practice of physical economy, such a return of the thus-increased talent, is manifest, *as a natural product*, as the increase of mankind's per-capita power in and over nature. In art, it is called play, signifying the importance of the quality of play, which Shakespeare's character Hamlet recognizes, but can not embrace, a Hamlet who is, like his nation, self-doomed by his fear of play, his fear of that realm from which he thinks no traveller might return.

A true Classical drama is never composed for the purpose of providing mere entertainment. Every great drama was composed with irrepressible playfulness, but also in deadly earnest, as were: Dante's *Commedia*; Bocaccio's *Decameron*, written as a commentary on the tragic siege of the Black Death, then raging among

---

50. The boy, as usual, had hitched up his mule, and the day's ploughing was under way. A stallion and a donkey, watched from over the fence. Suddenly, the donkey began braying, ridiculing the mule. "What are you laughing at me?" said the mule. "Because, despite all your hard work, you will never have a child," the stallion intervened. The mule rejoined, "Who do you think is walking behind me?" From the mule's standpoint, it made perfect sense.

the leading wealthy families of Florence, across the river below; François Rabelais' ***Gargantua and Pantagruel;*** and, Cervantes' portrayal of the tragedy dooming the Spain of Philip II, ***Don Quixote***. Forms of play such as the Classical tragedies of Aeschylus and Sophocles, the Socratic dialogues of Plato, and the tragedies of Shakespeare and Schiller, were composed in deadly earnest, to provoke the cognitive processes of the actors and audiences, alike, to an awareness of urgently needed adoption of certain principles of statecraft, for the sake of the historically specific, successful solution, for an historically specific problem of that place and time: the successful continuation, and betterment, of the society represented by those audiences.

For example, Shakepeare's plays on English history, reflect the legacy of the studies of the overthrow of King Richard III, as passed down as a tradition through, chiefly, the work of the martyred figure of England's participation in the Golden Renaissance, Sir Thomas More. Thus, from the same vantage-point as that study of the transition from Richard III to Henry VII, Shakespeare composed a dramatic overview of two centuries of the history of England's place within Europe. This was put on stage as a series of dramas, from ***King John*** through ***Richard III***. This series of dramas is devoted, throughout, to a single subject, the actual lessons to be adduced from the history of England, from the accession of the Plantagenet allies of imperial Venice, through the revolutionary change in statecraft established under Henry VII. Schiller's dramas, in most instances, addressed actual historical situations, and, on reflection on the actual history so selected, were accurate representations of the crucial issues of statecraft posed in the real-life history referenced by the stage.

In such great drama as that of Shakespeare and Schiller, the object is not the type of impulse to entertain the vulgar appetites for sensual exhibitions, such as those of the "night club," pagan Rome's Colosseum, or mass spectator sports, nor to provide a vehicle for the narcissistic impulses of the actors like Sir Lawrence Olivier, or the sado-masochistic, existentialist impulses of a director toward playwright, actors, and audience alike. The function of great drama, is to make the issues posed by a moment of real history, come to life with great force, within the cognitive processes of director, actors, and audience alike. The crux of such Classical artistic composition and its performance, is the evoking of the specific quality of passion unique to a state of cognitive insight. It is the same quality of passion experienced by one who is engaged in bringing forth a validatable cognitive discovery of a universal principle.

Compare this with the case of the profound superiority of the so-called Negro spiritual to the banality and superficiality of so-called "gospel" singing, to say nothing of that axiomatic contradiction in terms known as "Christian rock." I am not an expert in the Negro spiritual, but I have the advantage of being presented with the essence of the matter by experts who have demonstrated their argument to me most efficiently; the case they make has two aspects, both of which are relevant to the point I have just made, above, on the subject of Classical drama.

In its raw form, the Negro spiritual as I recognize it, expresses the historically specific situation and experience of the slave. On this account, a certain authenticity of presentation is essential for a convincing result. The singer must put himself, or herself inside that slave, and sing in a way which touches the quality which Friedrich Schiller defines as the *sublime*. I compare this quality of the spiritual to the expression of the sublime in Schiller's ***Joan of Arc***.[51]

In the development of Classical drama, we must recognize chiefly two distinct levels of such drama. The relatively inferior form is typified by the Classical Greek tragedy. On this account, Plato was not only critical of the leading Classical Greek tragedians, but presented the alternative in the form of his intrinsically dramatic Socratic dialogues, which must be performed and heard as the drama they are, to master their cognitive content. With Plato's dialogues, we encounter a typification of the transition from Classical tragedy, to the higher principle of the *sublime*.

In reviewing the works of the world's greatest modern dramatists, Shakespeare and Schiller, in their respective entireties, we may trace an upward development in their work, from the level of tragedy, to the sublime. The case of Jeanne d'Arc illustrates the distinction.

In history, Jeanne d'Arc's passion contributes a crucial role to the subsequent freeing of France from the evils of the long reign and ruin under the alliance between Venice and its Norman-Plantagenet partners. Her sacrifice made the existence of a true nation of France possible; also, in fact, she contributed indirectly, but notably, to the proceedings leading into the great ecu-

---

51. Friedrich Schiller, "On the Sublime," in *Friedrich Schiller, Poet of Freedom*, Vol. III (Washington, D.C.: Schiller Institute, 1990), p. 255.

EIRNS/Philip Ulanowsky

A Schiller Institute performance of excerpts from Shakespeare's Julius Caesar. *Here, Brutus addresses the plebeian mob, after Caesar's assassination. Shakespeare's tragedies and history plays were composed in order to bring about an awareness of urgently needed adoption of certain principles of statecraft, for the sake of solving an historically specific problem of that place and time.*

menical Council of Florence, which was the central event of the Fifteenth-Century Renaissance. Jeanne d'Arc was not a tragic figure, neither in history, nor on Schiller's stage. Her sacrifice of herself for her mission, was not a tragedy, it was the achievement of the sublime, as Schiller does much to define and refine the notion of the sublime in history and in art. She rose to the sublime in the imitation of Christ crucified. She lived and died for all mankind, not only France, all this, as she insisted repeatedly, for His sake. In the drama, Schiller substitutes a fictional element for the crucial historical event which actually precedes her execution, but, otherwise, the drama is true to history in everything it claims to present.

The great achievement of the Classical tragedy, even as tragedy, is that it presents an historically specific moment of crisis in civilization, in which the fatal errors of the prevailing national cultures and leaders of the drama, are placed on stage in such a way that the audience may be induced to recognize the principled nature of the fatal error then reigning in that society and its relevant leading figures. However, although recognition of the moral unfitness to survive of both the culture of Hamlet's nation and Hamlet himself, is a great

and useful improvement of the moral and intellectual qualities of the audience, it presents the sickness, but not the solution itself. Its usefulness, is that making the audience conscious of the fact that an avoidable error in moral character of a nation and its leaders was responsible for the catastrophe, inspires the audience with cultural optimism, with the hope that it might willfully free itself from such folly.

With Jeanne d'Arc, both in real life, and on Schiller's stage, she acts in a course, where she spends her life, but does not waste it; she returns her talent to God, enriched. Therefore, she is no tragic figure, but a representative of the principle of the sublime, just as the outcome of Plato's Socratic dialogues, notably Plato's treatment of the figure of the judicially murdered Socrates himself, exemplifies the principle of the sublime in science, statecraft generally, and artistic composition.

See a certain likeness in the slave represented by the Negro spiritual. Out of that condition, he affirms his humanity and his trust in God, and thus touches the sublime. It is always a song of humanity, of the humanity being crushed by servitude, but a cry of humanity which will not be stilled.

Classical Music As Science

In the first aspect of Classical art, as typified by great drama and poetry, the benefit of Classical art is more directly identified. Persons who have been civilized by saturation with the greatest examples of such artistic composition, have relatively superior powers for competence in statecraft and related matters.

This brings us to the second aspect of Classical art, in which the relationship to statecraft is, with certain exceptions, of a less obviously direct quality. Music typifies this second aspect.[52]

---

52. Notable exceptions include Giuseppe Verdi's operas, as only typi-

EIRNS/ Stuart Lewis

A Schiller Institute concert "For a Marian Anderson National Conservatory of Music Movement," in 1994 in Washington, D.C. Performers are (left to right) Rev. James Cokley, George Shirley, Detra Battle, Kehembe (Valerie Eichelberger), William Warfield, and Robert McFerrin.

with cognitive passion, the actual circumstances of the Crucifixion, as a cognitive experience of the sublime. The scores as written, recommend the participation of a musically qualified congregation in singing the parts obviously assigned to them, to such effect that they are not spectators for, but rather participants in the event.

How that functions, and what Wolfgang Mozart and others did, in adducing the principles of Classical contrapuntal thorough-composition of Mozart, Haydn, Beethoven, Schubert, Mendelssohn, Schumann, and Brahms from Bach's discoveries in use of series of Lydian intervals, need not be examined in any depth in this location. What does need to be stressed, is that Classical composition, most notably that of Bach, Mozart, Haydn, Beethoven, Schubert, Mendelssohn, Schumann, and Brahms, as contrasted with their adversaries, the Romantics, such as Rameau, Liszt, Berlioz, and Wagner, and the hoaxsters Helmholtz and Ellis, was to define the means by which the use of well-tempered counterpoint brings out the quality of cognitive passion, and thus produces a composition which, if competently performed, represents a single unifying Platonic idea as the identity (e.g., the "monad") of the composition as an indivisible unit. In the best result, as typified by Beethoven's Opus 132 string quartet, or the last of Brahms' four hymns, the *Four Serious Songs*, is the achievement of a sense of the sublime.

The origin of this mode of musical composition, lies within ancient notions of Classical (sung) prosody used in poetry composition. It uses the natural well-tempering subsumed by the natural range of human speaking and singing voices, to derive a corresponding polyphony, and a principle of polyphonic development, derived from the principle of the Lydian interval as the pivot of a developmental feature of composition. The difference between Bach's well-tempering and those who seek to degrade it to equal tempering, is the same

In this second aspect, as through the work of Harry Burleigh and others, as Haydn, Beethoven, Schubert, Schumann, Brahms, and Dvorak applied the relevant principles of Bach's and Mozart's Classical contrapuntal composition to the folk-song of the British Isles and Germany, principally, the great composer employs his musical insight into the folk-song, or folk-song-like compositions, to polish the intention which needs to be released from the encumbering limitations of the original.

For comparison, consider the challenge posed by the attempt to perform either of J.S. Bach's two great passions, the earlier *St. John Passion*, and the later *St. Matthew Passion*. Both address a spiritual subject, the passion and crucifixion of Jesus Christ, as defined by the relevant Gospels. The object of the performance of each composition, is to inspire the participants to relive,

---

fied by those which are adopted from the tragedies of Shakespeare and Schiller. Mozart's *Abduction from the Seraglio*, *Marriage of Figaro*, *Don Giovanni*, *Magic Flute*, and *Clemenza di Tito*, and Beethoven's *Fidelio*, are musical dramas which are purely musical, and yet also Classical drama of political relevance to the historical specifics of both the nominal setting of the drama and the audiences for which they were composed. The religious music of J.S. Bach, Mozart, Haydn, and Beethoven also typifies the integration of drama and music in an integrated way, not as a musical setting of text, but a qualitative, creative transformation of the delivery of the text to a higher dimension.

difference expressed by Kepler's exposure of the incompetence of the mechanistic, reductionist method of Ptolemy, Copernicus, and Brahe.

Similarly, in Classical plastic art-forms, the most important development, is that which existing evidence traces to the Classical Greek developments in sculpture, as distinct from the preceding Greek as well as Egyptian Archaic. Here, the subject is presented to the mind as in mid-motion, rather than as "tombstone" carvings. The revolution in perspective, established by Leonardo da Vinci, has a relationship to Classical Greek sculpture, but is a revolutionary scientific development in art effected during the course of the Fifteenth Century as continued into the beginning of the Sixteenth Century, and as echoed by Rembrandt.

Those background observations now supplied, the point to be made in this report, is that Classical artistic composition is defined as the development of methods for bringing the same cognitive principle required for generating a discovery of a valid universal physical principle, into its corresponding form of application to the study and representation of those social processes of cooperation among persons on which the successful promotion of physical-scientific progress depends.

In the literary non-plastic art-forms, notably Classical drama and poetry, the political side of the social function of Classical composition is explicit. Similarly, Leonardo's **The Last Supper**, and Raphael's **The School of Athens** and his **Transfiguration**, are examples of work which is purely Classical art, but also has a powerful political and scientific importance for statecraft, as I have indicated the general nature of that above.

A few more glances at the case of Classical musical composition, will round out that picture as much as is needed for this occasion.

The subject is now *metaphor*. The example chosen is *Classical thorough-composed song*, as typified by the new form of song-composition developed by Mozart, as expressed in his setting of a Goethe poem, **Das Veilchen**, as that new approach to song-composition was continued by Beethoven, Schubert, Mendelssohn, Schumann, and Brahms, most notably.[53]

Metaphor is the name, in literary composition and song, for a form of poetical *irony* which is termed *Anal-*

---

53. John Sigerson and Kathy Wolfe, eds., *A Manual on the Rudiments of Tuning and Registration*, Book I (Washington, D.C.: Schiller Institute, 1992).

ysis Situs in mathematical physics. It is the immediate juxtaposition of two or more mutually inconsistent statements, or individual terms, to define an idea which exists outside the bounds of consistency within the medium of representation employed in communication: *a dissonance*. It is to be compared with the case of Fermat's counterposing a description of reflection to refraction in terms of the language intended for representing events in what is imagined to be a Euclidean space-time.

Fermat's exemplary, concise juxtaposition of those two contrasted statements, both in the same form of description, implicitly destroys the credibility of a so-called Euclidean mathematics of physical space-time. So, Kepler, asks, what is the *Mind*, the *intention* of the planet Mars which causes its orbit to lie in a pathway not calculable within the framework of the Aristotelean notions of space-time commonly used by Claudius Ptolemy, Copernicus, and Brahe. To make that point, Kepler measures the orbit of Mars by means consistent with those of Euclidean mathematical statistics, and gains a result which is implicitly anti-Euclidean.

J.S. Bach approaches the issue of defining the proper tuning of musical instruments in a way which echoes Kepler's **Harmony of the World**. This comparison is demanded by a direct contrast of well-tempered values to those erroneous, so-called equal-tempered values, which a soulless mechanical man might estimate by use of an electronic hand-calculator. As I have already stressed here, the right value of the interval in a well-tempered composition, like the right value for the future velocity and position of a planet in its Keplerian orbit, can not be mechanically predicted as the systems of Copernicus and Brahe would suggest, or the methods of attempts at equal tempering.

The right value for well-tempering arises from the relations among what are called the natural register-shifts of each species of singing voice, among *bel canto*-trained groups representing the standard chest of *human singing voices*. In short, well-tempering is not defined from a so-called instrumental standpoint, but from the standpoint of certain ironies intrinsic to *bel canto vocal polyphony*.

To understand the problem, it is sufficient to throw out all notions of a theory of instrumental composition and performance, and recognize that the Classical performance of the musical instrument, must be an expression of the idea of the human singing voice, that musical instruments are intended to be echoes of the principles of the *bel canto*-trained human singing voice.

This brings us to Wolfgang Mozart's great discovery, as expressed in a series of compositions typified by the Köchel Number 475 keyboard ***Fantasy***. This composition represents Mozart's reworking of a celebrated J.S. Bach composition, the so-called ***A Musical Offering***. That Bach work, as complemented by the posthumously published ***The Art of the Fugue***, is a concentrated expression of one of the most important revolutionary features of Bach's work. Mozart's intensive Vienna study of Bach's work, led him to a discovery which not only revolutionized all Classical musical composition after that, but which is the most frequently quoted musical idea within the work of all leading Classical composers after that; the kernel of the discovery is expressed by that playful K. 475 ***Fantasy***. Mozart made explicit Bach's increasing reliance on a principle of musical composition, and play, associated with the term "Lydian interval."

To get directly to the essential point of relevance for this present report, focus upon the role of the method of *Analysis Situs* intrinsic to Bach's art of well-tempered counterpoint.

Take an interval of two tones, and now state that interval in an inverted order. State both of these juxtaposed intervals in the same key signature, and do so in a way which expresses the natural dissonance inhering in such a notion of inversion. If the development of that germ is successful, the attempt to resolve the counterpoint will lead inevitably toward a series of what are called "Lydian intervals," as Beethoven's famous Opus 132 ("Lydian") string quartet illustrates this, or the Brahms Fourth Symphony derived from a germ in the slow movement of Beethoven's Opus 106 "Hammerklavier" sonata.

The implicit dissonance in well-crafted choices of inversions, has the same effect as Fermat's resort, in counterposing reflection to refraction, to what Leibniz later named *Analysis Situs*. These metaphors, whether in mathematical physics or Classical artistic composition, define germ-ideas, as provoke that cognitive "energy" which requires the mind to make the cognitive leap from reductionist schemes, to discovering the cognitive principle which overcomes the apparently insoluble paradox so posed. That, in music, as in practice of mathematical physics, constitutes the identity of a Platonic form of *idea*.

When a great composer employs that principle of inversion, by such devices, to that purpose, his con-

science requires him to do nothing which does not introduce and develop that idea in such a way, that the development of the entire composition reaches a conclusion which defines the idea which the composer has chosen to bring into being through the introduction of the root-metaphor generated through inversion. If the composition is well-crafted, then it becomes the performer's duty, to deliver the performance of the composition in a way which never spoils the indivisible unity of the idea embodied in the composer's intention. Such a principle of performance was sometimes termed by the conductor Wilhelm Furtwängler, "playing between the notes."

Such was the stroke of genius expressed in Mozart's pioneering ***Das Veilchen***. Instead of setting the poem to the natural prosody supplied by the custom of the language used, as J.F. Reichardt did, follow the advice of the poet Friedrich Schiller, apply the principle on which Beethoven, Schubert, Schumann, and Brahms agreed with Mozart and Schiller, contrary to the argument of Reichardt and Goethe: discover a single musical idea, which shall control the singing of the poem from beginning to end, and use the implications of the Lydian principle in composition, as a way of making the sung prosody march to the idea which the poem itself is intended to express.[54]

The same intention is found, and made undeniably obvious, in the great artist's performance of the Negro spiritual, even when the means used by the artist may differ, in a formal sense, from the German Classical *Lied*, for example.

Complement the argument I have just given for music, with frank assessment of the decadence in the art of speaking which usually contrasts literate English speakers of my generation, to the "up-talk" and comparable perversions in habits of speaking, or of reciting text induced by recent or current, immoral idiosyncrasies of public school and university instruction, especially in reciting prose passages or poetry aloud publicly, among those of the "Baby Boomer" or later generations. The loss of the habit of Classical poetry, the Classical dramatic stage, and Classical music, has been a crucial factor in the loss of ability to communicate ideas among comparable representatives of later generations.

The person who speaks in a literate Classical mode,

---

54. ibid., Chapter 11, "Artistic Beauty: Schiller versus Goethe," passim.

speaks as one *who can be heard actually thinking,* rather than merely engaged in a more or less arbitrarily stylized recitation of what is either written, or memorized text, or a text the speaker is, in effect, writing as he goes along. The modern tendency is comparable to the case of the musician who is so busy interpreting the score itself, that he, while in that virtually schizophrenic state of mind, has no perceptible intellectual connection to the music which the composer intended.

The problem of speech typified by the increasingly illiteracy of manner of speaking among post-war U.S. generations of university graduates, in particular, is comparable as a problem to the case of the trained musical performer, who can play notes, without any understanding of music beyond the conventions which he or she recognizes almost as programmed instructions for note-playing. It is often worse than that; they "improve" the dish by putting tabasco sauce on the raspberry ice cream, so to speak. They read text in such idiosyncratic styles in text-reading; they do not oblige the prosodic utterance of the statement to conform to a process of development of ideas. Worse, they, as the Romantics do, add interpretation to text as such, without regard to the cognitive processes required by the clearly adducible intent of the text itself. They become functionally illiterates of that sort.

The same pathological state of mind is exhibited by the person who, when challenged to debate his, or her statement socratically, responds by repeating the statement more loudly, more angrily, perhaps adding the unsanitary proposal, "Read my lips." The victims of that perversion do this even in the case that the criticism itself exposes the statement being repeated as absurd. Why does that person exhibit such pathological behavior? The explanation is elementary: "It is my opinion!" and therefore has the attributed authority of the believer, of being *self-evidently my opinion.* One is reminded of the state of mind lurking behind the glaring eyeballs of that maniacal pre-middle-aged tail-gater, searching for her own shortcut to Hell, along the Maryland and Virginia highways of the greater Washington, D.C. region.

The relative impairment of the ability to communicate ideas, in the manner a Classical education and practice provide the relevant contrary standard, becomes a loss of the ability to think clearly, a loss of what the poet Shelley describes as the power of "communicating and receiving intense and impassioned conceptions respecting man and nature."

Culture As Education

As the case of Classical drama typifies this connection, all knowledge of statecraft is best developed through emphasis upon educating the young in both Classical approaches to physical science and Classical forms of artistic composition. The Classical form of study and practice of physical science, as I have indicated in this report, combined with a Classical artistic education, serves as the foundation for a competent grasp of the general problems and purposes of cooperation in general, and of matters of statecraft more narrowly. To complete the picture: the science of physical economy, properly bridges the roles of both science and Classical art.

The obligation of Classical humanist education, is to employ an historical approach to the cognitive apprehension of the history of scientific and Classical-artistic ideas, to the purpose of building up within the student's memory, his, or her own equivalent of the kind of sense of a simultaneity of eternity, as I outlined the case of Raphael's *The School of Athens.* The pupil should relive the history of ideas, historically and cognitively, to that effect.

The intended result, is that the student should locate himself, or herself in a great span of human history, as one in direct communication, cognitively, with the living minds of the greatest original thinkers of that past. The development of the personal character of the student, in this mode of education, tends to ensure a beneficial result which could be achieved in no other way. In brief: as the student defines the student's personal relationship, through the methods of the Socratic dialogue, to living notable persons long since deceased, so the student is impelled to come to see himself, or herself, in respect to those who have yet to be born. It is that manner of development of the moral character, so defined, of the pupil, which is the only proper central aim of education.

The motivation of the pupil must become, concern for the consequences which the present bequeaths to the future, a generation or more ahead. There is nothing arbitrary in this. To transform a newborn child into a young adult, requires approximately a quarter-century of development. During that quarter-century, the expenditure of effort and means on the development of the young individual, brings no net return on that expense. Important projects of development take years before reaching the point of yielding net economic fruit. Yet, what will happen a quarter-century ahead, will be deter-

EIRNS/Susan Welsh

Youngsters explore the heavens through the "Mysterium Cosmographicum" telescope, made by Schiller Institute member Charles Hughes, at an Institute festival in honor of "underground railroad" leader Harriet Tubman in Auburn, New York.

mined, often, by the decisions chosen today. As in the case of Kepler's meticulous measurement of the orbit of Mars, the velocity and position occupied by that planet tomorrow, will not be determined by the statistical trend adduced from its recent movements. Science must always locate the long-term expression of the intention embedded in the process being considered.

It is not possible, except in an oppressively stagnating economic culture, and perpetually decadent society, such as that prescribed by the Code of the Roman Emperor Diocletian, to determine what a young person in school today should be doing a score of years ahead. The choices available then, will depend upon a combination of the decisions made beforehand and in between. What we can know with reasonable certainty, is the degree of general development, and related adaptability we should seek to build into the labor-force as a whole. Rather than training the person to fit the specific form of employment (which, by that time, should no longer exist), develop the economy to make use of the quality of labor-force we are working to develop.

It is the level of development which the present generation will make possible for its successors, which should be the determining consideration in economic policy today.

Beyond all other considerations, educational policies must be conditioned principally by the consideration, that the function of education, is to produce qualified citizens of a true republic, with no substitute for that allowed in defining educational policies of practice. The primary responsibility of the citizen, is not that of an employee, but, rather, a policy-maker for society as a whole. It is to that end, and no other, that goals for the education of the individual are to be chosen. Nothing less than the fulfillment of that goal shall be a minimum standard of education of the future adult member of society.

Once it is agreed, without exception, that that is the universal mission of all education, we can consider other things, but without eliminating, or depreciating any part of the obligation to serve education's primary mission-responsibility.

This does not place an excessive burden on the educational system. The presently practiced modes in education are immensely wasteful of the time and energy of the pupils. Heave out the popularized rubbish, to save time and energy for what is of more durable value.

As I have indicated here already, there are really two essential departments in required forms of education: 1.) Mankind's relationship to the universe, in physical terms; 2.) mankind's relationship to mankind, and person to person within society. Both departments are, and must be situated in history apprehended cognitively as a simultaneity of historical eternity, as this must be provoked into existence within the mind of the student. Stick to that business, and discard the clutter which is commonly substituted for education in today's educational institutions.

Take astronomy, for example. For many cognitive exercises a pedagogical laboratory capability is needed. Very little is required, by comparison, for an introduction to astronomy. The universe is there, an astrophysical reality which serves as a demonstration experiment relentlessly continuing its motion. It is that, the great demonstration experiment, up there, called astronomy, ocean navigation, geodesy, and so forth, upon which the most ancient of societies, whichever they were, first produced the rudiments of what we recognize as physical science today. "With your bare eyes and some sticks and stones, proceed to construct a calendar. Don't admire the stars; don't waste your time just mooning and gawking, when you might be engaged in beginning to construct a calendar. Don't look it up on the Internet; know what you are talking about; look up to the stars, instead."

Keep what I have identified as the principles of cognitive education in focus. The practice of learning must be superseded, to a relatively enormous degree, by a thoroughly cognitive, historical approach to education, as my references to the example of Raphael's *The School of Athens* typify the point. The historical, direct and personal link, through cognition, of the minds of the original discoverers from the past, to the students, must be the foundation of all pedagogy. The students must be engaged in the cognitive passions of an endless Socratic dialogue with all notable minds from the past. All knowledge is located in the importance of experimental validation of the hypotheses developed in response to the ontological quality of paradoxes expressed within the bounds of that realm of relative simultaneity of eternity.

On this account, the structure of public and university education must incorporate a relatively great emphasis on the facilities for, and activities of pedagogical proof-of-principle experiments. The notion that any hypothesis must be validated, and that in the direct cognitive experience of the students, must be the rule, whether the replication of a past discovery of universal principle, or testing of the mastery of the lessons of that experience, in pioneering into the experimental domains of fundamental research to the purpose of discovering new universal physical principles, and discovering new kinds of technologies which may be derived from those principles.

This also means a certain upper limit on average class-size, and the training and placement of teachers and other relevant specialists in the amount and quality needed for such a program. In the end, these changes in the program and its budget, will cost the U.S.A. (in particular) less than nothing. The increase of the harvest will vastly exceed the added costs of the program. The principle is, that the only source of increase of the average productive powers of labor in society, is the increase of the rate of production and assimilation of more advanced knowledge of universal physical principle, and of the new technologies spawned as offspring of such discoveries of principle.

This implies a sweeping recrafting of the entire primary and secondary curriculum, and correlated changes in programs for universities, too. That requires a great effort. That effort is not only worth the expenditure; it is now indispensable for the survival of civilization.

4. European Civilization

Up to the present day, we have no reasonable choice of dating available, for the first appearance of the human species on this planet. We can only estimate, that that must have begun in the order of millions of years ago. The best evidence to date, is fairly consistent with the general retrospective picture given by Plato's *Timaeus*, which points toward the conditions under which what we regard presently as historical times, emerged, during the closing, melting phase of the preceding 200,000 years or so of the most recent general glaciation of the land-mass of the Northern Hemisphere.

To supplement that information, we have cave paintings from scores of thousands of years before the present, which show a much higher level of culture than most current cultural anthropologist's standard mythologies would allow to exist, and we also have crucial evidence dating from some hundreds of thousands of years earlier than that, of a cognitive human individual, no mere higher ape, existing in Europe.[55]

On the deeper issues of scientific method posed by this subject, the implications of Vernadsky's case for the "historical" self-development of the biosphere and noösphere, respectively, give us some useful parameters. Two sets of observations to such effect, matters on which I have reported in earlier locations, should be sufficient to situate the way in which we should approach the subject of the recent approximately 2,500 years, since the emergence of European civilization on the foundations provided chiefly by the legacy of ancient Egypt. Look at the matter from this vantage-point, and then turn to the immediate political setting of U.S. education today, the matter of European civilization's development as so situated.

First, as to the existence of the human species as such.

---

55. See Renate Müller De Paoli, "Die Höhlenmalerei der Eiszeit," *Neue Solidarität,* Feb. 23, 2000; Hartmut Thieme, "Lower Paleolithic Hunting Spears from Germany," *Nature*, Feb. 27, 1997, pp. 807-810; Robin Dennell, "The World's Oldest Spears," *Nature*, Feb. 27, 1997, pp. 767-768.

To situate the existence of mankind with respect to the phenomena of both European civilization in general, and globally extended modern European civilization as well, let us box in the issue of the origins of human life, by aid of the following observations, once again, on the implications of the work of Vernadsky.

The issue of tracing the origins and development of human life on Earth, must begin with the fact that the uniquely cognitive form of life, mankind, exists. Not only must human existence have begun at some point in the development of the Earth's biosphere, but certain preconditions, within the biosphere as a whole process, had to have been satisfied for that emergence of man to have occurred.[56] Inevitably, for many, the most shocking, even stunning implication of Vernadsky's portrait of both the biosphere and the noösphere, is that what he cites as his experimental evidence, points implicitly to the appropriate dating of the occurrence of a principle of life, and also of a principle of cognition, as located in whatever might be considered the beginning of the existence of the universe.

To restate that crucial last point, if life is not derived, in fact, as by evolution or otherwise, from a universal physics of non-living processes, and if *life is,* as Vernadsky argues experimentally, *a demonstrably efficient, universal physical principle in its own right,* then, *life always existed* as a principle of our universe. *The same kind of experimental proof applies to the principle of cognition,* which, among all perceptible phenomena, was, from the beginning, unique to those human forms of life which emerged later.

Then, the appearance of the existence of a living species which is characteristically cognitive, the human species, signifies that the preconditions for the appearance of the already waiting principle of human life, had then been realized, that in a certain degree and quality of the development of the biosphere in general. It also indicates, that within the specific features of organization of that living process which is the human individual, there exists something to be discovered, which corresponds to the appropriateness of the human species for cognition, an appropriateness which is lacking in the higher apes.

Moreover, it follows from this, that since, as our na-

tional "melting-pot" experience in education exemplifies this, all human beings have the same kind of cognitive potential, then, on this account, it follows, that all human beings are of the same species, and, when defined by that specific cognitive distinction, are of the same race.

These distinctions, among three respectively unique classes of universal physical principles, are associated with the corresponding, specific ranges of relative anti-entropy, as expressed among each of those three classes of universal physical principles. This is demonstrated, with relative great emphasis, by the effect of human intervention in accelerating the anti-entropic development of the biosphere, as this is shown by including the human species and its specific activity as a biological part of that biosphere as a whole. This entails the consideration, that the durability of the existence of a species, depends upon its enjoying *the level of rate of attributable relative anti-entropy associated with, and required for the perpetuation of its own existence.*

In the case of the only known cognitive species, the human species, its superior anti-entropy is expressed by those cognitive aspects of formal and other education, which transmit accumulated discoveries of principle, as from the past, into the mental processes of the living.

Meanwhile, to understand what this anti-entropy represents, and to shape policies to the effect of promoting it, we must discard the Clausius-Kelvin mythology, respecting thermodynamics. We do this on the basis of what should be the obvious, conclusive epistemological evidence, that the root argument in support of their claims, does not actually reflect crucial scientific evidence as such. Rather, as the reductionist's axiomatic fallacies of Grassmann's and Boltzmann's mathematics illustrate the point, it reflects the superimposition upon the physical evidence, of the hereditary influence of purely arbitrary, reductionist types of axiomatic mathematical assumptions. They made the same hereditary type of reductionist error which Descartes perpetrated on the matter of *vis viva,* and Ptolemy in astronomy.

In that case, our view of what we regard as the non-living aspects of our universe, must define development in the alternative terms of the emergence of relatively higher orders of anti-entropic *organization,* as primary, and the phenomena of relative energy-flux density are to be judged as derived from a universal

---

56. I do not mean evolution in the empiricist's sense. I mean the existence of man as a cognitive species, requires preconditions, knowledge of which has yet to be determined, within the biosphere as a whole process.

physical principle of organization, as Leibniz's principle of the monadology expresses this conception, rather than the ideological reductionists' insistence on interpreting the experimental evidence the other way around.[57]

In that latter case, the notion of universal entropy, is discarded into the black museum where all superstitions and other biological freaks should repose, there to warn future mankind against repeating such follies. Instead of axiomatically reductionist thermodynamics, we must regard as primary, the different orders of relative anti-entropy to be considered in assessing the relations and distinctions among apparently non-living universe, life, and cognition. In that case, the universe we inhabit, then becomes, to say the least, much more interesting.

So much for situating a discussion of the preconditions for human existence. Now, turn to the second point, as to the emergence of modern civilized forms of human life.

The earliest evidence of the existence of what we call scientific culture today, is passed down to us in the form of ancient astronomical calendars, such as those known to us from the period of the building of the so-called Great Pyramids of Egypt. The study of these calendars from the standpoint of modern science, shows that these include cycles which reflect cultures of far greater sophistication than can be explained as products of relevant known cultures dated from early within historical times. That is to say, that much of the astronomical and related traditions known from early within historical times, is, like the lunatic contemporary fads of astrology, demonstrably a vulgarized and superstition-ridden parody of actually scientific work from within earlier, so-called prehistoric times.[58]

We must not underestimate such scientific achievements from within the so-called prehistoric times of the last great ice-age on the northern hemisphere's land-mass, but we must not overrate the moral qualities of the cultures of those times, either.

As the case of ancient Greece attests, some ancient societies have contributed a rich legacy of intellectual contributions, at the same time they treated the majority of the related human population, as Sparta did, among others, as actually or virtually human cattle. Chattel slavery in modern European civilization, is but a specific expression of the bestiality of man to man which was characteristic, in more severe or relatively milder degree, of every historically known society from every part of the world. The myth of the "noble savage," or of the moral "beauty" of cultures which actually never existed outside classroom and other mythologies, must be relegated to the same black museums in which the existence of deadly diseases and past experience with oligarchs and biological freaks, is kept on record as a warning to future times.

For these reasons, combined with considerations I have addressed in earlier locations published in the course of decades, the earliest traceable civilizations are to be found among transoceanic maritime ("Peoples of the Sea") cultures, such as the Dravidian language-group's maritime culture, which introduced civilization, as its colony of Sumer, into lower Mesopotamia, and the trans-Atlantic cultures whose Indo-European language-group branch settled in post-glaciation Central Asia, and contributed its cultural legacy to areas including the Iran and Indian subcontinent of today.

During the latter phase of the melting of the great glaciation that had sat for so long upon much of the northern hemisphere's land-mass, the oceans had risen by 300-400 feet above their earlier levels, the great periods of devastating flooding had came to a close, and a process of civilizing parts of the more accessible coastal and major riparian areas then proceeded. As the maritime traits of certain calendars indicate, civilization did not move from inland to the oceans, but the reverse.

---

57. In knowledge, as cognitive generation of the ideas of universal physical principle are generated, a paradox of the type of *Analysis Situs* always defines the fact of experience from which knowledge of universal principle is derived. When such knowledge is configured as Riemann's principle implicitly requires, physics, so defined, presents us with a multi-connected architecture of the universe, its *organization* as to matters of principle. It is the view of the universe as a self-organizing process, from this standpoint, which shows us what the evidence as such permits us to consider as "elementary," and what not. Hence, organization-as-such, so defined in principle, must replace notions of self-evident discrete magnitudes. Then, consider Planck's discovery as correlated with the notion of a monadology, rather than self-evidently elementary particles as the reductionists define them. Notably, as emphasized implicitly by Kepler's success over the reductionist methods of Claudius Ptolemy et al., the attempt to derive physical principles from within the bounds of a mathematics based upon reductionist assumptions, is the hereditary principle which separates all constructs in formal logic fatally from science.

58. Typical is the case of the hoax perpetrated by the Roman Claudius Ptolemy, who fraudulently reworked the heliocentric constructions of his Classical Greek predecessors, in service of the method of Aristotle. Repeatedly, societies based upon the oligarchical model, perverted the results of earlier astronomy, as a matter of producing myths used as instruments of social control over the minds of the population.

Even to this day, as the condition of the so-called "Great American Desert," Central Asia, Africa, and the heart of South America attest, the process of making inland areas of continents as accessible to the development of physical economy as coastal and major riparian regions, has been far from completed.

Those two considerations, the one scientific, the other representing some relevant, broad-best estimates, situate the emergence of the history of civilization in a general way. However, one additional point must be heavily emphasized, before taking up the emergence of European civilization upon foundations which were supplied, to a large degree, from Egypt.

The Indomitable Human Spirit

The best examples of the Negro spiritual as such, express that essential quality of all mankind, on which a competent education policy must be premised, as if axiomatically. As long as mankind exists, the essence of human nature, the cognitive principle, can not be stilled. Thus, as history affirms Plato's calling attention, as in his *Timaeus*, to the verifiable fact of many cases of destruction, or self-destruction of cultures before his time, there has arisen, repeatedly, from within mankind, the force of that indomitable spirit of cognition, to give a new birth to the hope of achieving a durable civilization.

In fact, as Plato emphasizes, entire cultures have been swept away, either by natural catastrophes beyond mankind's control at that time, or by a tragic error embedded within the self-doomed culture itself. The case of the super-Krakatoa-like explosion which demolished ancient Thera, is but one example of natural catastrophes. The self-destruction of the Mesopotamian and Roman empires, typifies cultures which collapsed because they lacked the moral fitness to survive. Yet, after such catastrophes, the impulse to give society a new birth, has expressed itself somewhere, sooner or later, sometimes with manifest, if but partial success. To give the best examples of successful renewals of a failed culture, a scientific name, call these, exhibitions of the universal principle of the renaissance.

The Fifteenth-Century, Italy-centered Renaissance, which created a revolutionary new form of society, the modern sovereign nation-state premised upon the principle of the general welfare, is the most important example of the universality of the indomitable human spirit in action.

In history, there is usually an essential conflict between the influences welling up from the human spirit, and the contrary characteristic impulses of the culture which that population inhabits. The cognitive principle is a natural human impulse, naturally specific to the individual member of our species. It is the principle of goodness, the quality which defines all newborn persons as intrinsically, redeemably good by nature. However, in every form of society known, even within the U.S. today, for example, the prevalent tendency of the culture is that expressed by the degradation of a very large part of the population to the condition, and sense of personal identity, which is fairly described as characteristic of human cattle. There sits the principle of evil.

The innate goodness of the individual person, his, or her cognitive potential, is, generally speaking, always there, and will express itself if the cognitive impulse is not suppressed, or corrupted in other ways. From case to case, such spontaneous expression is more or less difficult. Some oligarchical cultures are less unfavorable to cognitive expression than others. Those poets and scientists who express the Classical approach to composition, rather than the opposing Romantic approach, or something like it, are a measure of the degree to which the spirit of freedom, otherwise called cognition, has found moments of escape from the oppression which otherwise prevails in that culture, that society.

The case of the development of Classical Greek culture, Plato and his Academy most notably, typifies the relatively happier developments to such effect.

Sometimes, all the noted evidence suggests, that some admirable piece of creative expression, such as the Negro spiritual composed amid the conditions of slavery, springs into being without any connection to the work of some earlier period of Renaissance. However, we know that no creative thinker works without a strong impulse to reach into the more or less distant past, or some distant place, in search of predecessors or contemporaries with which he might identify in a way akin to our John's and Robert's study of the discovery by Archimedes. So, ancient, medieval, and modern European civilization maintained connections of that sort to Classical Greece's legacy.

So seek in all distant and past places, likely spoor of the good, but also attempt to situate the place of the occurrence of that good in its appropriate, actual place in the historical process as a whole. This brings us to focus upon the unique global historical significance of the successive impact of the cultural revolution which occurred in Classical Greece, and, its successor in that Fifteenth-Century European Renaissance which gave birth to a revolutionary new kind of institution, the modern sovereign nation-state premised upon that principle of natural law called the general welfare.

In Plato's Socratic dialogues, and in the Christian view, the combat against that evil of oligarchism, is the imposition of what is properly called *natural law* upon government, to serve what is called by such names as "the common good," or "the general welfare." That Socratic principle, called *agapē*, was adopted from the Classical Greek of Plato by Christianity, as typified by the Apostle Paul's *I Corinthians* 13. Although that term, translated into Latin as *caritas*, and thence into English as "charity," is often degraded into the giving of kindnesses, such as forbearance, by the ruling oligarchs to the human cattle of society, such as British ladies teaching the Irish poor to hang lace curtains in their windows, Paul's contrary meaning of the term is clear, as is Plato's.

However, despite the principle of Christ and His Apostles, it was not until the Fifteenth-Century Renaissance, that a putatively Christian western Europe acted to create a new form of state, the sovereign nation-state, under that rule of natural law known as the general welfare. Even then, the oligarchical faction in Europe, typified by the far-flung imperial maritime power of Venice and its instrument, the Habsburg oligarchy, drowned Europe in orchestrated religious warfare, during much of the 1511-1648 interval, in the effort to eradicate the pioneering forms of nation-state first introduced as that of France's Louis XI and England's Henry VII. Since the close of the Seventeenth Century, within globally extended modern European civilization, the newly established British monarchy and the legacy of the Habsburg faction, has continued its efforts to eradicate the principle of the general welfare, and to turn the world back, forever, to modern echoes of ancient and medieval oligarchical imperial models of world government, as over the course of the Twentieth Century, and still today.

In the U.S., past and present, the anglophile alliance of Manhattan-centered predatory finance-capital and the tradition of the Southern slaveholder interest, usually acting so in concert with the British monarchy, has maintained the oligarchical tradition to the degree it has

A "conspiracy" for the General Welfare: Benjamin Franklin (left), with other authors of the Declaration of Independence: Jefferson, Adams, Livingston, and Sherman.

been able to do so, both inside the U.S.A. and in our nation's foreign policy of practice. This continuing struggle between good and evil, the republican commitment to the general welfare, and the anglophile commitment to the evil of oligarchical interest, has been a dominant feature of educational policies and practice within the U.S.A. itself.

That is what must be changed. Reforms of the usual this or that will accomplish virtually nothing good in the end. The evil can not be tamed with meliorative reforms; it must be uprooted. To uproot it, we must impose an appropriate form of what is for today, a revolutionary change of governing principle in national educational policy of practice. To accomplish that, we must know what we are doing. That means that we must locate the unique significance of the modern sovereign form of anti-oligarchical nation-state, as summoned by the 1776 U.S. Declaration of Independence, in history as a whole.

To understand that, we must know how good conspiracies work.

The Christening of the Idea

Nothing constructive in shaping history could be brought into being without a good conspiracy.

Among literate people, "conspiracy" means what a strict etymological-historical reading of the term suggests. People who agree to act in concert according to

The "conspiracy" to create European civilization, expresses an impulse for changes in the axiomatic assumptions respecting the conception of man. Here, an ancient Greek amphitheater.

certain common axiomatic kinds of assumptions, are conspiring in the most literal meaning of the term. The U.S. Declaration of Independence and Preamble of the Federal Constitution define active conspiracies. However, be cautioned, that to agree to do an act, would be a crude and inelegant literary pretense, which would not, in and of itself, meet the standard for literate use of the term "conspiracy." The term should be used to signify the case in which people agree to cooperate, chiefly in actions yet to be determined by them, but in service of the realization of some set of axiomatic-like principles, such as those, once again, reflected in the 1776 U.S. Declaration of Independence and the 1789 Preamble of our most fundamental constitutional authority on law, the U.S. Federal Constitution, with its included "general welfare clause."

So defined, conspiracy as such is neither good nor bad, and may be either good or bad. There is nothing bad in conspiracy as such. Judges and prosecutors often conspire against defendants, for example, and sometimes, in cases well known to me from my studies, the defendant's attorney shares in that conspiracy. That is bad; but, conspiracy is also an indispensable way of bringing about all public good.

The most relevant historical example of a good con-spiracy, is the manifest transformation in the image of man, which is traceable from the beginning of the Homeric epics, through the full-blown emergence of Classical Greek culture in the work of Plato and his Academy. The most significant changes are of an axiomatic quality, changes in the set of axioms expressed as ideas about man in the universe.

The most interesting phase of that process of change, begins some centuries before the judicial murder of Socrates by the Democratic Party of Athens, in the sponsorship of the Ionian Greeks and the Etruscans, as allies of Egypt's combat against the so-called Phoenicians. The long alliance of the Babylonian and Persian Empires with Tyre, against Egypt, the repeatedly unsuccessful efforts of the Persian Empire and Tyre to crush Greek civilization, and the destruction of both Tyre and the Persian Empire by forces led by Alexander the Great and his advisors from the Platonic Academy, are the pivot of a great conspiracy, on which the definition of the emergence of European civilization, as European civilization, depends.

Think of the emergence of European civilization as a prime example of a true conspiracy. This conspiracy does *not* take the form of the planned attempt to impose some "blueprint" upon reality, but like the ***Odyssey*** of Ulysses, expresses *an impulse for a certain direction of successive changes in axiomatic assumptions of practice respecting man, his conception of the reigning gods, and his relationship to nature.*

For the world as a whole today, the most interesting mythic figure of the ancient Greek epic as a whole, is the ironical role of a putatively Egyptian goddess imposed upon the Olympic pantheon as the figure of reason, Athena. The direction of those successive changes, approximately culminating in the establishment and work of Plato's Academy, is the emergence of the Classical humanist conception of man.

The impelling force of this process of change, was

the insurgency of what I have identified as the indomitable, cognitive human spirit.

This was not a mere epiphenomenon of those we know retrospectively as the ancient Greek population. It was a conspiracy within that population, a conspiracy which was able to impose its mark on the ancient Greek heritage for later times with such force, that many people forget that those who introduced those changes were, like the circles of Benjamin Franklin, revolutionaries within their own times and among their own people. These changes were, like all truly good changes, revolutionaries of the type associated with the validated discovery of a universal physical principle by the initiative of an individual and the support for that by a relatively small group associated with the work of that individual. This is as appropriately a model of the best creative artists as of physical scientific discovery.

Great good conspiracies are of the type to be recognized in the relationship of Leibniz follower Abraham Kästner to his student and collaborator Gotthold Lessing, and the close collaboration of Lessing and Moses Mendelssohn, as defenders of the work of both Leibniz and J.S. Bach, against the circles of Voltaire and Leonhard Euler of the Berlin Academy. The same is true of the continuation of the German Classic, as organized in that form by the initiatives of Kästner, Lessing, and Mendelssohn, which gave the world the German Classic of Goethe, Schiller, the Humboldts, Scharnhorst, Mozart, Beethoven, Schubert, Heine, et al. These changes occurred within societies which were, otherwise, predominantly expressions of the anti-Classical Romanticism of Immanuel Kant, G.W.F. Hegel, Novalis, et al., just as the evil, oligarchical Delphi cult of the Pythian Apollo, typified not only Lycurgan Sparta, but many among the contemporaries of Greece's greatest and noblest Classical figures.

The central feature of the centuries-long process leading into the establishment of Plato's Academy at Athens, was a struggle against, and within the grip of the existing pagan religious beliefs of that time and place. Two overlapping expressions of evil, are of the greatest relative importance: the cult of Olympus and the Delphi cult of the Pythian Apollo. It is important to capture a sense of the revolutionary character of the figures of both Ulysses and Athena, relative to the setting of the Olympian myths.

Like the mind of the majority of the U.S. electorate today, the minds of most of the populations of known societies have been controlled by the use of fraudulent kinds of religious superstitions. These have been superstitions of a frankly religious character, such as the Olympus cult and Apollo cult, or in ostensibly secular disguises for religious belief, such as British empiricism, existentialism, astrology, the escapist mystique of mass popular entertainment, and "the market." All taken together, they constitute a body of *ideology*. By ideology, I signify a system of belief which is adopted by learning or kindred, axiomatically irrational methods, such as the belief that humanity's fate is controlled by the whims of supposed gods of Olympus.

In conventional U.S. practice, ideology is expressed typically by a certain way of using the pronoun "they," as to signify some eerie "establishment," of which it is said, "they will always decide." Granted, as long as eighty percent or more of the U.S. population continues to behave in that superstitious way, as it has in recent general elections, for example, as virtual human cattle herded into the allotted pens, a relatively small number of people, operating through their lackeys, will rule the U.S. pretty much as the most pathetic true believers among the ancient Greeks believed in the absolute power of the ever-whimsical gods of Olympus. It is useful to see the U.S. population today, as exhibiting the most pathetic features of the subjects of the *Iliad*.

It is useful to compare the *Iliad* and *Odyssey* on this account, and to trace the changes in man's conception of himself as expressed by Solon's reforms at Athens, by the Classical tragedians, and by Plato's figure of Socrates. Such false gods rule only as long as the people allow this state of affairs to prevail, as long as the people fasten the shackles of humility toward such would-be, or even purely imaginary gods, such as "The Invisible Hand," upon themselves.

What emerges in this progression from the Homeric epics to Plato, is the shift to the concept of what becomes, in Plato, the *idea*, as the adduceable principle of Classical Greek sculpture's difference from the Archaic, presents the image of the idea as reflected in the language of stone, the idea of *becoming-in-motion*. The figure of Ulysses already introduces a willful evocation of an idea in the hearers of the song of the *Odyssey*.

The poem of Solon presents the idea of the idea with great force. The Classical tragedians Aeschylus and Sophocles, are most notable. Plato and his figure of Socrates, represent the pinnacle of this Classical Greek achievement. The notion of *agapē*, as elaborated in the *Republic*, for example, goes to the heart of the matter.

Throughout the span from Homeric epics to Plato, there is an unfolding process at work, a process which returns always to the issues of justice and truthfulness, these as the alternative to credulous submission to belief in "they," the alternative to submission to "popular opinion," to submission to a reigning ideology. In the end, the work of the Socratic dialogue, in defining the Platonic form of ideas as the standard of justice and truthfulness, becomes, ever since, the quality which sets the emergence of European civilization apart as the birth of a distinct culture, and which provides the foundations for what became the characteristic distinctions of the Fifteenth-Century Renaissance.

The destruction of the Persian Empire by the hand of Alexander the Great, established the leading position of the Platonic legacy within the Hellenistic culture of the eastern Mediterranean and its associated regions, which continued until the Romans had defeated the Greek states in Italy, and moved on to conquer, and largely enslave Greece itself.

Pagan Rome, which expressed both the legacy of the syncretizing cult of the Pythian Apollo and of ancient Babylon's oligarchical model, became the long nightmare of European civilization, from which Europe could escape only through an affirmation of the Classical Greek alternative to Romanticism. This affirmation occurred through the embedding of the Classical Greek legacy of Plato within Christianity, to an effect typified by the Fifteenth-Century Renaissance.

So, in the form of a continuing conflict, over thousands of years, between the Classical Greek and Romantic legacies, the continuity of European civilization has been established as of a distinct type, up to the present day. It is impossible to achieve any effective comprehension of the internal history of today's now globally extended European civilization, except from that standpoint. The Classical Greek legacy was thus christened to become the most powerful form of culture known to date, not merely by some standard of raw power, but on account of the power expressed by the use of the method of the Platonic idea.

The corollary is, that the world was fated to bear the burden, and the advantages, spilling over from the continuing, millennia-long, great conflict between the Classical and the Romantic within European civilization. Such has been the christening and the aftermath of the *idea*.

The Birth of the Sovereign Nation-State

Now, to sum up with the following crucial, concluding point.

To understand the now globally extended history of European civilization over the past two millennia, it is sufficient to begin by recognizing, that the terrible conflict within European civilization could be overcome, only by eliminating the oligarchical model. That means, today, uprooting the Venetian model of an imperial financier-oligarchical form, in which the reign of a policy sometimes called "shareholder value" degrades virtually all of mankind to the condition of herding, consuming, and culling, the great mass of the population as a human cattle, as has become the increasing practice inside the U.S.A. since the Richard Nixon "Southern Strategy" campaign of 1966-68.

For this end, of freeing humanity from an oligarchy's degradation of the mass of the population to the status of the virtual human cattle which the great majority of the U.S. population suffers today, it has been nec which, by implication, outlaws oligarchical practices. That law has two features. First, that the authority to rule over a nation must be given only to sovereign governments of nation-states. Second, that no government has the moral authority to exist, except as it efficiently promotes the general welfare of all of the people and their posterity: the common good. In all matters, that principle of the general welfare must be accorded the authority of the highest law applicable to the case at hand.

This was the great change sought in the battles fought by the Emperor Frederick II against Venice and Venice's Plantagenet allies. This was the great end sought by Dante Alighieri's proposed reforms. This is the great fruit of the Fifteenth-Century Renaissance. This is the principle under which Louis XI's reform of France occurred, and Henry VII's uprooting of the evil represented by the Plantagenet legacy of Richard III. This is the source of the unique quality of the intention applied by Benjamin Franklin and his collaborators to the creation of the U.S.A. This reform is modern European civilization. This is the unfinished business, which we must bring to a conclusion.

In this unfinished business inside the U.S.A. itself, policies governing the general practice of education, form a leading, crucial part. For historic and related reasons, the policies of education and related perspectives for employment of our so-called African-American families are a kind of acid test. Often embittering, and bloody experience of our nation shows, that if we are either unwilling, or incapable, to bring about a reversal of the legacies of chattel slavery and so-called "Jim Crow," as it applies to education, the nation and most of its people will continue to walk, as they have done lately, like serfs or slaves, bearing their shrunken heads on their shoulders.

The power of a nation's real economy lies entirely in the combination of the development of the cognitive maturity of its people, and in the provision of those forms of organization and conditions of life and work, which are the circumstances required for production and for general life by any level of advancement of the scientific and technological capabilities of the minds of the individual members of the labor-force and their families. The higher the level of development, and latitude for expression of the cognitive powers of the individual, the greater the average power of the economy as a whole, the greater the rate of progress of the human condition.

Do not fit the development of the people to the perceived requirements of forms of employment deemed available. Rather, transform the policies of investment in employment, to set priorities on the utilization of the greatest feasible development of the labor-force and its family households.

Indeed, it was never the lack of opportunity to upgrade employment opportunities, which prompted racists to condemn African-Americans into tracking (of most among them) for menial employment and worse education. They were racists, because they were oligarchs, who understand that if a people is not stupefied in relevant ways, it will not endure rule by oligarchs. Therefore, the oligarchs prefer to keep people dumb and deluded, and also culled as much as is deemed convenient, even if that means a much poorer performance for the economy, because it is more important to them to be oligarchs, than to allow that far more successful form of economy, in which free, thinking men and women, will not tolerate being human cattle for oligarchs.

The object of sane economic policy, is to develop the cognitive powers of all the citizens to the highest possible level they are willing to achieve, and to compose the conditions of production and distribution to keep pace with the progress achieved through such policies of reliance on Classical humanist education for each and all.

We must give priority on this approach to education and employment prospects, and to developing the means to conduct such a policy of practice. Only when all means "all," in these terms, will the legacy of racism dwindle away. Only when we do this for ourselves, and reflect this in relations with other nations, will our nation's prolonged gut-pain of racism pass away.

FIDELIO

Journal of Poetry, Science, and Statecraft

From the first issue, dated Winter 1992, featuring Lyndon LaRouche on "The Science of Music: The Solution to Plato's Paradox of 'The One and the Many,'" to the final issue of Spring/Summer 2006, a "Symposium on Edgar Allan Poe and the Spirit of the American Revolution," *Fidelio* magazine gave voice to the Schiller Institute's intention to create a new Golden Renaissance.

The title of the magazine, is taken from Beethoven's great opera, which celebrates the struggle for political freedom over tyranny. *Fidelio* was founded at the time that LaRouche and several of his close associates were unjustly imprisoned, as was the opera's Florestan, whose character was based on the American Revolutionary hero, the French General, Marquis de Lafayette.

Each issue of *Fidelio*, throughout its 14-year lifespan, remained faithful to its initial commitment, and offered original writings by LaRouche and his associates, on matters of, what the poet Percy Byssche Shelley identified as, "profound and impassioned conceptions respecting man and nature."

Back issues are now available for purchase through the Schiller Institute website:
http://schillerinstitute.org/about/order_form.html